A Concise Dictionary of

Cumberland Dialect

based on William Dickinson's *Glossary of Cumberland Words and Phrases*

Edited by Richard L. M. Byers

FIRST PUBLISHED in November 2006 by
Landmark Librarium (an imprint of Richard Byers)
based on William Dickinson's *Glossary of Cumberland Words and Phrases* - last published in 1905

RICHARD BYERS
Fletcher House, 136 Moresby Parks
Whitehaven, Cumbria CA28 8XH

www.richardbyers.co.uk

ISBN 0 95384479X (softback)
Landmark Guide # 03/001

British Library Cataloguing in Publication Data
A catalogue record of this book is available from the British Library.

ERRORS and OMISSIONS
Whilst the greatest care has been taken in the preparation of this book, the author cannot be held responsible for any errors or omissions.

INTRODUCTION

THE NATIVE FOLK-SPEECH of *'Oald Cummerlan'* has many of its roots in the Norse and Old English tongues, and is a peculiar language that once proved almost intelligible to people living beyond the borders of the county. Although many words are still commonly heard across Cumberland (which now forms the northern section of Cumbria) this book will reintroduce some of the old, lost and forgotten words and phrases to present generations.

William Dickinson's first *Glossary of the Dialect of Cumberland* was published in 1859. Twenty years later a second edition appeared with major additions and revisions. Earlier in 2006, I produced a comprehensive dictionary with over 7000 entries, based very much on that edition Also included was the work of E.W. Prevost who revised Mr. Dickinson's dictionary in 1900 and 1905. Over a century has now past and copies of the original books are scarce and very much sought after. This book is a concise (or laal) version of my larger dictionary, but still contains upwards of 800 words and phrases.

Please do not view this dictionary as merely another studious book for the intellectual. It can and should be enjoyed by every member of the Cumbrian household. In a spare moment, either alone or with family and friends, reach for your copy and delight in its contents. Reciting just a few extracts will surely bring a broad smile to your faces.

I feel extremely privileged to have followed in the footsteps of Mr Dickinson almost a century and a half after his first dictionary was published. My task of editing this augmented work for todays reader presented me with a wonderful opportunity to fully explore his unique contribution to the study of Cumbrian etymology, linguistics and local history. The debt which Cumberland owes to William Dickinson is a heavy one, and it is my hope that this new edition will give his work the wider recognition it so richly deserves.

Richard L. M. Byers
October 2006

READERS NOTES

ANYONE who has studied Cumberland dialect will be aware that many words often vary considerably in their pronunciation, spelling and even meaning as we move from district to district across the county. Mr Dickinson reflected these geographic variations by adding a key letter to an entry where it had particular regional significance.

Basically he believed that the county could be divided virtually horizontally into three distinct zones. The italic letter ***C*** following a word or phrase refers to the central area, essentially that part of the county lying between Aspatria in the north and Egremont in the south. Above this zone is the northern area, denoted by the letter ***N***. Likewise the region to the south is referred to by the letter ***S***.

Sometimes further variations occur across one of these three main areas and are indicated by using key letters such as ***SW*** and ***NE***, which obviously refer to the South West or North East and so on. As the Borrowdale area has many of its own unique words or phrases, the letter ***B*** is used to highlight these entries. Where no italic letter follows an entry, that particular word or phrase is (or once was) in general widespread use across the county. The letter ***G*** is also used to indicate a general entry where appropriate.

Dialect however, has really no clearly definded boundaries and will often shade into and blend with its immediate neighbours. This occurs not only regionally, but also further afield. To the south of Cumberland, the words and the mode of pronunciation and expression gradually merges into those of the old counties of Lancashire and Westmorland. To the north into the Scottish regions of Dumfries and Liddesdale and to the North East into the distinctive Northumbrian dialect .

ACKNOWLEDGMENTS

The author wishes to acknowledge with grateful thanks the kind assistance and contributions offered by Jo E. Byers, Amy M. Byers, Natalie D. Byers, Andy V. Byers, Ted Relph (of the Lakeland Dialect Society) Michael Burridge, Whitehaven Record Office, Carlisle and Workington Public Libraries. Furthermore access to the works of the late E. W. Prevost , S. Dickson Brown and several others has proved invaluable and essential inorder to do the work justice.

Aa *C* I. *'Aa fell't ower the dog.'*.
Aa *N, SW* all; of; owe; own.
Aa'd I would; I had.
Aa'l I will.
Aa'z I is, I am.
Aakart *SW* awkward.
Aalas *SW* always.
Aald *SW* old.
Aalwas *N* always.
Aapral *C, E, SW* April.
Aariddy *SW* already.
Aawgust *C, E, SW* August.
Aback behind.
Abeun *C, E* above; more than.
Abe-nn *C* above.
Abide *C, SW* to bear, stay, remain, suffer, withstand.
Aboot about.
Adveyce *NW* advice.
Afear't afraid.
Afeut *C, E* afoot.
Afe-tt *C* before.
Afoor *C* before *'It'll rain afoor neet.'*; in front of; in preference to.
Afore *N* before.
Afword *C, E* afford.
Afwore *E, N, SW* before; in front of; in preference to.
Ageann again; against. *'I's nut ageann yer plans to wed, but yer fadder is.'*; before.
Agyen *NE,* **Agin, Agyan** again.
Ah I.
Ahint behind.
Airm *N* arm.
Airy breezy. *'It's rayder airy to-day.'*
Alang along.
Alean, Aleann alone.
Aleb'm *C, E, SW,* **Aleeven** *C, N* eleven.
Allus *N* always.
Ally a narrow lane; the aisle of a church.
Alongsides *C* beside.
Am him. *'Catch am an' hod am, an' whack am weel.'*
Amang among.
Ameasst, Ameast *C, SW* almost.
Ameeast *N, E,* **Amyast** *C* almost.
Amiss used in slight (negative) approval. *'it's nut seah far amiss.'*
An 'ing' - as a terminative. eg. *'Risan'* - Rising.
An *G* one, eg. *'baddan'* - bad one.
An' *C* and. *'Ham an' eggs fwoor oor teas.'*.
An' o' also, and all, too. *'We'd breed an' butter an' cheese an' o', an' o' maks o' drink.'*
An' all *W* as well. *'Dick's fray Cockermuth an' all.'*.
Aneuf *C,* **Ane-gh** *NE,* **Aneuff, Anew** enough. *'Ah knew Dick's oald fadder weel aneuf.'*.
Ang-ry vexed; applied to a sore it means inflammed or painful. *'That's an ang-ry bile on t'leg.'*.
Anither *N,* **Anudder** *C, E* another.
Anny *SW* any.
Anonder, Anondyr under; beneath
Anoo *SW* enough.
April fe-ll *N,* **April gowk, April noddy** *C* April fool
Are ye middin weel? a greeting meaning *'How are you?'*.
Argify to debate or argue.
Argy argue; signify. *'It doesn't argy'* - it does not signify
Arse abuett feass back to front; all wrong; topsy-turvy.
Arse end backside or bottom.
Arsewurts backwards.

Arsin abeutt to fool about; to turn around.

As how *C* that. *'He said as how he wad nivver gang near them.'*

Aside *C* beside; near to. *'Parton aside Whitten.'*

Ass *C* ask; inquire.

Ass ask; ashes.

Ast asked; did ask.

Asteed instead.

At that

Atween between

Aw *C* our.

Awivver however, *'Awivver, we knea yer fadder's nivver rang.'*.

Awtagidder *C* all together.

Awwer *SW* our; hour.

Awwt *SW* out. **Awwtin'** *SW* an outing, pleasure trip or jaunt.

Ax *C, E* ask; inquire. *'Find oot what udder fwokes are axin, before yer selt it.'*.

Ayder either.

Aydle *C* to earn. **Aydlins** earnings.

Ayont *NW* beyond.

Ayqual *SW* equal.

Aywas *C, N* anywise; always.

Baa *SW* ball.

Baal, Baald *N* bold, imprudent.

Babblement silly discourse or talk.

Babby baby or small child.

Back bake.

Back end *C* the autumn season. *'On about t' back end.'*

Back shift the second shift worked down a mine etc., generally 2pm to 10pm.

Back word a countermanding or a change of mind. *'They ax't us t' tea yaa day, and than they sent us back-word.'*

Backa beyont *C, N* a far away, often isolated place.

Bad beukks out of favour. *'I's in yer Mary's bad beukks, fwor doing nought.'*.

Bad fettle poorly or ill.

Baddan *C,* **Baddin** *N* bad one; the evil one.

Badder worse. *'Many a badder thing med happen.'* **Baddest** worst. *'It's t' baddest thing 'at could hev happen't.'*

Badly *C* poorly; ill; out of health.

Badly off poor.

Baggish luggage; also a term of reproach to a child or a female. *'a dirty baggish!'*

Bagwesh *C* poverty and destitute. *'He's gone to bagwesh.'*

Bain *C, NE* handy, *'Yon's ti bainest way.'*; willing.

Bairn *N* a child, a term of familiarity.

Bait lunch, meal or snack; formerly a feed for a horse while travelling.

Baith *N* both.

Ban *NE* band.

Band bind.

Bang to beat; to excel; an act of haste. *'He was bad to bang.'* *'He com in wid a bang.'*

Bannish *N* banish; forbid the house.

Barfet *C* feet naked, without shoes.

Barn *C, SW* a child. *'Oor lass is still at heamm wid t'barns.'*.

Barn time *C* pregancy in women.

Barra wheel barrow.

Bash away!, Bash on *C, NW* work vigorously; strike hard.

Bassenthet *C* Bassenthwaite.

Bat a blow; a stroke; the sweep of a scythe.

Batter to slope; to incline; to beat; to attack with repeated blows. *'That girt lad batter't oor laal Jack.'.*

Bawnce, Bawwnce *SW* bounce.

Bawnnd, Bawwnd *SW* bound.

Baww *SW* bow, bend.

Beak, Beakk *C,* **Beeak** *SW* bake.

Beak *N* nose.

Beann bone.

Bear *C, SW* , **Bearr** *C* bore; did bear.

Beath, Beatth *C, SW,* **Beeath** *N* both.

Beatt abate; did bite. *'Our dog beatt a lump out o' t'oald busy bodys hand.'*

Bed bid or bade. *'They bed o't'parish to t'berryin'.'.*

Beek *C, N* to heat or bake.

Beel *C, N* to bellow; to brawl.

Beel *N* boil.

Beeldin' *N* building.

Beer to bear.

Begon began.

Behadden *N,* **Behodden** *C, SW* beholden, obligated.

Behint behind. *'I's nut far behint yer.'.*

Bela' *SW* below.

Belangs, Belengs belongs.

Beleev believe.

Bellar to use bellows on a fire; to shout. **Bellars, Belliz, Belluz** bellows.

Bellican *C* an obese person or animal.

Bellt *N* bald.

Belly flapper, Belly flopper a poor dive into water, landing flat with a blow to the stomach.

Belyve after a while. *'Aa'l pay thee belyve.'.*

Benk *C* a low bank or ridge of rock; a bank or finance house.

Bensal *B* violent motion. *'He com wid a bensal.'*

Bensal to beat. *'Aa'l bensal ta'* - I'll beat thee.

Bent *C* bleak. *'Yon's a bent pleass o' yours.'*

Berryin' *B* a funeral.

Best bib and tucker on *B* said of a female in a very fine dress (1878), later also used to refer to a well dressed male in his best suit or *'sunday best'* outfit.

Bet betted, did bet: did beat.

Better *C* more. *'Theer was better ner twenty.'*

Bettermer of the better sort. *'The bettermer swort sat snug in the parlour.'* - Robert Anderson.

Betterness improvement. *'Theer nea betterness in t' weather yit.'*

Between whiles at intervals.

Beuk *C, N, E,* **Beukk** book.

Beur *C, N* bore, did bear.

Beurd beard.

Beut *C, N, E* boot. **Beutless** *C* bootless.

Beutts boots.

Bever *E* tremble.

Bew bough or branch of a tree.

Beyble *NW* bible.

Beyd *N, NW* to abide etc.

Beyont, Beyout beyond.

Beyt *NW* bite.

Bid to invite.

Biddable obedient; tractable.

Bidden *C* occupied; taken.

Biddy *C* nursery name for lice, differnt speices infest the bodies of humans, animals and plants; term often applied to a cantankerous woman. *'Yer Marys a oald vile biddy.'.*

Bide *C, SW* to abide etc.

Biggan *N, SW* the act of building. **Biggin'** building.

Bile *C, E, SW* to boil; a sore inflammation or swelling.

Bin *N* been.

Binch *C*, **Binsh** bench.

Binna *B* be not.

Bisky biscuit.

Bit *B* small or little. *'A bit buoy.'* - a little boy.

Bit *C* but, *'Yon field grows nought bit bent and pry.'.*

Bit but; position or station life, *' He's pinch't to hod his bit.'.*

Bit *N* little. **Bit thing** *N* small or insignificant.

Bittock *N* a bit.

Biz'ness *C* business, *'A good stroke o'biz'ness.'.*

Bizzen *NE* ugly or ill-natured; shameful.

Bizzin' *B* buzzing as bees; busy at work.

Bla *N*, **Blaa** *SW* blow.

Blaa out *N* an often excessive drinking or eating session.

Blab to let out or reveal a secret or an indiscreet talker.

Blabberskite *NE* a vain-talking fellow; an indiscreet tell-tale.

Black kites *C* wild bramble berries.

Blake pale yellow, *'Blake as May butter.'.*

Blare *C* to roar violently; to bellow.

Blash to splash.

Blashy poor, weak, *'That Workin'ton yal nut blashy.'* or *'Mary maks blashy tea.'.*

Blead, **Bleadd** blade.

Bleaken, **Bleakken** blacken.

Bleam, **Bleamm** blame.

Bleary *C* windy, cold and showery.

Blebs *C* bubbles; watery blisters

Bleckon'd *B* blackened; the skin discoloured by a bruise.

Bledder the bladder; to talk nonsence.

Bledder *N* to roar violently; to bellow.

Bleeak *SW* bleak.

Bleeat *SW* bleak; bleat.

Bleeze blaze.

Blenk *C, N* a gleam, *'A blenk o' sunshine.'.*

Blether *N* idle talk.

Bleud, **Bleudd** *C* blood. *'Sum o'them gat gay bleuddy feasses.'.*

Bleum, **Bleumm** bloom.

Blin *N* blind.

Blind man's holiday evening twilight; darkness.

Bliss *G, N* bless.

Block to strike or hit; the head, *'I'll knock thee block off.'.* - blocks are used in hat making.

Blonk *C* a blank, *'Jack's got duble blonk.'* - double blank at dominoes.

Blow to let out a secret; to spend money fast, often with little thought.

Blur blot; to defame.

Blurt *C* to tell or speak out something unexpected.

Bo *C, E* ball.

Bo man *C* an imaginary person used to frighten children, eg. boggle.

Boddam bottom; low ground; a small valley or hollow; to empty. *'He could boddam a quart at a wind.'.*

Boddamest the lowest.

Bodder bother. *'Yer lad bodders about nought.'*.

Bodderment perplexity, distraction, confusion or anxiety.

Boddersom troublesome.

Boddom bottom.

Body *C* person, *'This het weather an' hard wark fairly ups a body.'*.

Boggin very dirty.

Boggle *C* ghost or bogeyman.

Bogie sledge on wheels,small cart.

Bogie whol *C* a small cupboard or store, often filled to the brim with seldom used items.

Bok *C* the motion in the throat when attempting to vomit from nausea.

Bonnily prettily. **Bonny** beautiful, handsome, *'Ho er ye to-day, bonny wee Jack?'*.

Boo *C, N, E* bow, bend.

Booak *SW* book.

Booal *N, E, SW* bowl.

Booat *SW* boot.

Boogle *NE* see Boggle.

Book bulk. **Booksom, Booky** bulky.

Bool *C, N* to bowl, as in cricket etc; boldly. *'Bool in lads.'*.

Boonce *C, E, N* bounce.

Boonmest *SW* uppermost.

Boot a bout; a turn; a contest; an entertainment.

Borst *N* burst.

Botch to mismanage, make a mess of job or task. *'Thou has mead a botch on 't now.'*.

Bound days see Beunn days.

Bowt bought, did buy. *'Ah bowt yan off him.'*; a bolt.

Bowze *B* to rush out, as blood when a vein is cut.

Braid *NE* broad. **Braid** *NW* to spread; to throw about.

Braith *N* breath.

Brak broke.

Brake *B* a break on a wheel.

Brake *C* to beat.

Brandreth *C* an iron frame for supporting the baking-plate or girdle at a proper distance above the open fire; a trivet.

Brandreth steann *C, B* a boundary stone at the meeting of three townships or parishes.

Brang *C, SW* brought.

Branglan' *NE* wrangling.

Brannigan *C* a fat puffy infant boy.

Brant *C, SW* steep. *'As brant as a hoose side.'*.

Branthet *C* Branthwaite.

Brash *C* rash, headlong. *'He's a brashan' body, and runs heid and neck still.'*.

Brash *E* a spell or turn of work. *'Kursty, come kurn a brash.'*.

Brashy *C* weak; delicate.

Brass copper money; riches; impudence; assurance. *'He's plenty o'brass in his feass.'*.

Brast burst.

Brat *C* a contemptuous term for a troublesome child; a coarse apron. **Brat** noisy, cheeky or naughty child; to spay - a young ewe is bratted to prevent it having a lamb.

Brattle the loud rattling noise of thunder, etc. **Brattle can** *C, B* a noisy child. *'Mary's sec a la'al brattle can.'*; a kicking cow.

Brave superior; fine; of a good sort. **Bravely** *C, NE* quite well. *'I's bravely, how's thou?'*.

Bray to beat or strike; chastise and

bruise, mostly in reference to children.

Braythet *C* Braithwaite.

Brayzent *C* brazen; impudent; excess of assurance.

Brazzle *C* to press into a crowd, etc.; to scorch or singe.

Breaa *SW* brow, to its limit or boundary. *'T'beck's breaa full.'.*

Breadd *SW* broad.

Break to beat with a stick (used chiefly as a threat), generally applied to boys. **Breakk** *C. SW* to thrash; to beat

Bree *B* in a great hurry, *'In a girt bree.';* joyous or uplifted. **Bree** *NW* good. *'He's no bree.'.*

Breead *SW* bread.

Breeak *N* to beat.

Breeast *SW* breast.

Breed *C, NE* bread. *'Cut thy sel a shyve o'cheese an' breed.'.*

Breeght *N* bright. **Breet** *C, SW* bright.

Breeth *C, E, SW* breath.

Breeze *N* bruise.

Brek *C* to break; fun; a practical joke. *'Sek breks!';* a good story.

Brek break.

Brekfast *C* breakfast.

Brekkan *C* breaking.

Breme *NE* to froth. *'It bremes ower'* - it froths over the brim.

Brent *N* steep. *'As brent as a house side.'.*

Brenth breadth.

Breum broom or brush; the broom plant *Sarothammus scopari.*

Breuz *C, E,* **Breuzz, Briss, Briz** *C* bruise.

Brig bridge.

Brist *C, NE* breast.

Brist burst.

Brither *N* brother.

Brock broke or broken, *'He fell off t'oald byre an' brock his leg.';* a badger. **Brocken** broken.

Brong *N* brought.

Broo *C* brow; to its limit or boundary, *'T'beck's broo full.'.*

Broon brown.

Brossen *C, SW* burst.

Browse *C* friable; mellow. *'You may begin to sow, for t'land's browse now.'.*

Browte brought.

Brudder brother

Bruffle *B* excitement.

Brulliment *N,* **Brully** *C* broil or cook over hot coals; disturbance or noisy quarrel.

Brunt, Brust *C,* **Brussan** *N* burst. **Brussen** *B* burst, overworked.

Brussel bristle.

Bruz *C* bruise.

Bu bough, branch.

Buck up *C* to subscribe; help or assist; to advance. *'Buck up till her, lad.'.*

Buckel't *C* A saw is *buckel't* when it is over-bent, or a wheel is *buckel't* when its rim is bent and bowed.

Buckle *C* order; condition; health. *'He's l'girt buckle today.'.* **Buckle** *C, SW* to marry; fasten upon; attack. **Buckle** to attack and seize.

Buckle teah begin; take in hand. *'Buckle teah, men, ye're varra welcome.'.*

Budder brother.

Buff nakedness. *'Strip't into buff.'.*

Bum to be furiously busy. *'Bumman about like a bee in a bottle.'.* **Bum** *SW* see Bumbaily.

Bumbaily bailiff; a sheriff's officer. *Billy Bumley* house on Workington's foreshore was a Customs officers look out point.

Bumly *C* the humble-bee, *Bomba.*

Bummel *C* to bungle; blunder.

Bummel kites *N,* **Bummelty kites** *E* wild bramble berries.

Bumper a large one.

Bun *N,* **Bund** *C, E* bound.

Bunce *N* bounce.

Buoy *B* boy. *'Johnny sec a la'al buoy.'.*

Burk birch.

Burn *N* brook, rivulet, streamlet or watercourse.

Burnt his fingers applied to persons having failed in some object, or having been over-reached, lost money through careless investment. *'Tommy's burnt his fingers at shopkeepin'.'.*

Burr *C* a sudden hurry *'He went off wid a burr.'.*

Burth birth. **Burthday** birthday.

Busy body one who to enquires into others affairs and tells tales. *'Yer Mary's summat of a busy body.'.*

Butty a sandwich; bulky at the butt or lower end, *'like oald Bennett wife.'.*

Bwoat *C boat.*

Bwore *C, SW* bore, did bear.

Bworn *C* born. **Bworn days** *C 'In o'my bworn days.'* - in the whole course of my life.

By-set *C* anything set aside till wanted.

Bye by.

Caa *N, SW* to call; scold; proclaim. *'T'kurk clark co't'a seall.'.*

Caald *N, SW* cold. *'It's parlish coald.' 'Ey, fit to skin a teadd.'.*

Caan't *C, E,* **Caat** *SW* cannot.

Caaw *B* to walk with the toes turned inward.

Caaw't twisted; said of shoes when worn down on one side.

Cabbish cabbage; to purloin or steal. A plagiarist cabbishes.

Cad *C, SW* to mat or felt together. *'Her hair was caddit till it cud niver be cwom't mair.'.*

Cadge to beg or borrow.

Caird *N* card.

Caleever *E* energetic and ungraceful action. *'He's a caleeveran' dancer is Jack.'.*

Callas't *C* hardened skin; calloused.

Caller *N* fresh, cool.

Cam *N* came.

Can *C* able or can, *'I'll nut can gang to-day.'* - I am unable to go. **Canna** *N* cannot.

Cannel candle. **Cannel-leet** candlelight. *'When harrows begin to hop, cannel-leet mun stop.'....'Efter oald Cannelmas neet ceukks find cannel-leet.'.*

Canny a term of praise or encouragement. *'Canny Jack! lig at him till he nivver giz in.';* pretty, nice, suitable, gentle; cautious. *'Be canny.'.*

Canny bit an uncertain term of comparison; as *'a canny bit better'...'a canny bit warse.'..*

Cant to overturn; to lean to one side. *'It's gitten a cant to ya side.'.*

Canty merry, lively, cheerful.

Cap't to surpass or better something, to overcome. *'He's fairly cap't now.'*; puzzled

Capper one who excels.

Cappers something difficult. *'Aa'l set thee thy cappers.'.*

Car reeght *N,* **Car reet** *C* cartwright.

Carf carve, *'Fadder, carf t'ham at t'teabbel.'.*

Carl coarse unmannerly fellow. *'A rough carl.'.*

Carry on, Carryin's on *C* to be playful or rompish. *'They'd fine carryin's on.'.*

Cassel *G, not E* castle.

Cassen *N* cast, overturned. (see Cassen).

Cat lowp in near proximity; *'within a cat lowp.'* - within the jump of a cat.

Cat-talk *C* idle conversation; small talk. *'Jack talk't nought bit a heap o'cat-talk.'.*

Catch't *G, not E* caught.

Catchy *C* capricious, apt to change suddenly.

Cause because.

Caw, Caww *SW* cow.

Cawm *G, not E,* **Cawn** calm.

Cawt *C* called.

Cawwnt *SW* count; account. (see Count).

Cawwrse *SW* coarse, course.

Cawwrt *SW* court; caught.

Cawwshin *C, E, SW* caution. **Cawwshious** *E, SW* cautious.

Cayshin *G, not E* occasion. *'Nay, thank ye, I've neah 'cayshin.'.*

Ceakk cake.

Cearr care.

Ceass case. **Ceass hardent** case hardened; insensible or unfeeling to shame or remorse.

Cessen *C, G,* **Cest** cast; overturned. *'Jack's car was cessen in a gutter.'.*

Ceukk cook.

Ceull *C, G* cool.

Chafts jaws.

Champ *C* to bruise or crush. *'He champ't his thoom in a yat sneck.'.*

Chance barn an illegitimate child.

Chap't *SW* cracked skin from cold or neglect.

Chase *NW,* **Chass** *SW* chase.

Chats *C* small potatoes; ash-tree seedlings. **Chattees** *C* potatoes

Chatter *C* to shatter *'Chatter't into splinters.'.*

Cheas, **Cheass** *N* chase.

Cheeap *SW* cheap.

Cheeat *SW* cheat.

Cheeny china ware.

Chern *SW* churn. **Chern't milk** *SW* butter-milk.

Chess *C, E* chase.

Chibies *N* onions.

Chiggle *C* to cut wood unskilfully.

Chimla *C, SW* chimney or flue.

Chip *C* to trip; a term in wrestling; the first breaking of the shell by the young bird.

Chitty feast baby faced.

Chock full *C* full to the top.

Chollers *C* fatty jaws and double chin.

Chooaz *SW, E* choose.

Chop to barter; to change. *'T'wind chops round t'north.'.*

Chops jaws. *'Aa'l slap thy chops for tha.'.*

Chowe chew.

Chowk *C, N, E* to choke or strangle.

Chris'mas Christmas. **Chris'mas**

box a gift or present given at Christmas.

Chufty *C* a person having fat cheeks; chubby.

Chunter *C* to reply angrily and weeping.

Churry *C, E* cherry.

Chwose chose, did choose.

Citty the wren; a receipt or order, delivery note or similar note on a slip of paper.

Clag to stick to. **Claggum** *N* toffee, (see Taffy). **Claggy** clammy; adhesive.

Clam did climb. *'Jack clam out at t'fell heed like a crow fleean.'*. **Clammer** clamber or to climb.

Clam up *C* stop talking; to satiate or fill up, feed to the full, to cloy or glut. *'Aa's fairly clam't up wi'sweets.'* .

Clap to pat; to squat as the hare does. *'Jack clap't his sel down on t'settle without iver bein'as't.'*.

Clap on *C* put on a lid or hat, etc.

Clart adhesive dirt; anything clammy; a scrap. *'He still leaves clart on his plate.'*.

Clartan *B* getting dirty or messed up; wasting time. *'Yer Mary's just clartan on.'*.

Clashy wet and dirty.

Clatter clogs *C* a noisy walker in clogs or pattens.

Clawt, Clawwt *SW* a blow; a patch; a rag.

Cleadd *C* to clothe, to cover or enclose.

Cleath *C, E* cloth.

Cleaz, Cleazz *C* clothes.

Cleean *SW* clean.

Cleeaz *SW* clothes. **Cleed** *N,*

Clethe *N, E* to clothe, to cover or enclose.

Cleg *C* the sting fly, *Chrysops.* To stick like a cleg is a common expression for a good or close adhesion.

Click *C, SW* to snatch; a steep part of a road. *'It's a sharp click up Workiton Ho'brow.'*.

Clim to climb.

Clip't *C* clipped; shortened. *'T'days is clip't in a bit.'*.

Clipper *C, SW* a clever one.

Clivver *C, N, E* clever. *'Jacks sec a clivver lad, fwor his age.'*.

Clog *C* shoe with wooden sole; a block of wood.

Cloggy fat and heavy. *'As cloggy as a fat su.'*.

Clom *SW* having climbed.

Clonter to walk clumsily and make a clattering noise with the feet.

Clooas *SW* close, hot; to shut; an inclosure

Clood cloud.

Cloot *C, N* a blow; a patch; a rag.

Clot *C, N, E* an idiot or silly person; a clod; to throw clods, etc. *'They clottit t'lasses wid apples and hed sec fun!'*. **Clot heed** a stupid person.

Clout cloth; clothes

Clowe *C, SW* to scratch; to beat. *'She gev him a clowin.'*.

Clower *C* a quick worker. *'A clowan knitter.'*.

Cludder *C* to crowd together; cluster.

Cluff *N* a blow.

Clwose close; hot; to shut; sultry. **Clwoze** *C* close; an inclosure.

Co' *C* to call, scold, proclaim, come.

'Jack co' towert me and I said cuh naa narder.'

Coald *C, E* cold. *'It's parlish coald.' ....'Ey, fit to skin a teadd.'.*

Cob to kick; to beat; a loaf of bread, often round in shape.

Cobble up to perform a task roughly and hastily.

Cock sure *C* confident; perfectly certain.

Cock-loft *C* top attic where cocks may have once been kept in cock-fighting times.

Cockelty *SW,* **Cockly** *C, N* unsteady or on a precarious foundation.

Cockermuth. Cockermouth.

Coddle cuddle or to embrace.

Codebeck *C* Caldbeck.

Coff *C, E* cough.

Col *N* cold.

Collaps, Collops scallops; slices of potato, usually pan fried in bacon fat or lard.

Colleckshun collection.

Com *C, SW* came, **Com** come.

Come calm.

Come ageann. pardon can you repeat what you said.

Come't *C* came. *'He's come't in.'*- He came in.

Conk *C* the nose or profile *'Oald Bob with t'howker conk.'.*

Connily *C, SW* prettily. **Conny** pretty, nice, suitable, gentle, cautious. *'Be conny,'or cautious.*

Coo *C, N, E* cow.

Coo clap, Coo skarn *C* the dung or droppings of the cow.

Coont *C* count. *'Coont t'things ower agean.'.* **Coontit** *C* counted.

Coor *C, N, E* cower, crouch.

Corkin' *B* a severe beating.

Corp *C, SW* to die; corpse.

Cot did cut; has cut. *'He cot his thoom wid his sickle.'.*

Cotter *C* to entangle; to mat together. *'It was cotter't like an oald wig.'.*

Count *C, N* count; account. *'I count nought o'sec wark.'* - I hold it in no esteem. **Countin'** counting; arithmetic. *'Jack! git t'countin' dun.'.*

Covver to recover. *'He cover't five pund dammish.'.*

Cowe *SW* to intimidate; to place in subjection.

Cowgh *N* cough.

Cowp to exchange.

Cowshin *C, N* caution. **Cowshious** *C, N* cautious.

Cowt colt; a petted child, *'Mother's la'al cowt.'.*

Craa *SW* crow; to boast in truimph, to swagger.

Craal *SW,* **Craawl** *C, N* crawl.

Crack a conversation, gossip, news - *'Come Jack lad, give us thy crack.';* to do quickly or succeed in a task. *'As will, in a crack.';* to boast; to restrain. *'He's nought to crack on, for he set his dog on a bit lad and wad n't crack't off ageann.*

Crack't not in his right sense. *'Theyne dog's crack't in t'heed.';* succeeded in a task.

Crackan *C* talking or chattering.

Crad, Craddagh *C* a troublesome child; an inferior animal.

Crag *C* the face; the neck or countenance. *'He hang a lang crag when t'news com.'.*

Crammel *C* to scramble; the walk

as if with sore feet.

Crammelly *C* tottery, unsteady.

Cranch *C* crunch; to crush with the teeth. Coarse sand cranches under the feet.

Crankelty *C* very crooked; zigzag; *'O'in's an'outs.'.*

Cranky crotchety; sickly and complaining. *'How's thy oald mudder?' ....'Nobbet varra cranky to-day.'.*

Crap *N* crept.

Crawl *E, SW,* **Crawwl** *SW* to crawl.

Crawwn *SW* crown; the top of the head.

Cree to crush or break into fragments. **Creein'** crushing.

Creelin' *E* cowering, crouching.

Crib *C, N* curb; the curb of a bridle.

Crinkelty *C* very crooked; zigzag; *'O'in's an'outs.'.*

Crippy *B* a stool. *'La'al Jack sit tha' on thy crippy.'.*

Cro *C, E* crow, *Corvidae*; to boast in truimph, to swagger.

Croab't *C* drunk, *'Oald Jonty's naa croab't agin.'.*

Crony *C, B, N* a comrade, friend, companion. *'Wudsworth and his gay cronys are out o' t'fells ageann.'.*

Crood crowd.

Croon *C, N, E* crown; the top of the head.

Croppen *C, SW* crept. *'He was lang varra wankle bit he gat croppen out ageann.';* failing in bodily appearance. *'T'oald woman's sare croppen in.'.*

Crottelly *C* crumbly.

Crowl *C, N, E* to crawl, *'La'al Jack crowl't onder t'teabbel.'.*

Crusty ill-tempered.

Cry *N* call, 'Cry the lad back.' or *'Cry in as ye come back.'.*

Cubbert cupboard

Cud *C* could. **Cuddent** *C* could not, couldn't.

Cuddy an ass or donkey. *'As't thee 'iver sin a cuddy lowp a five bar geatt.';* an idiot or simpleton.

Cue *C* trim; temper. *'He's i'girt cue to-day.'.*

Cuff *C, N* the back or nape of the neck; a blow on the head.

Cuh *C* come. *'Mary co'towert me and I said cuh narder.'*

Cum *C* come. *'I cum fra Workinton.'.* **Cum** a expletive frequently preceding a remark, etc. *'Cum! What hes ta to say?'.*

Cumman *C* coming. *'A reet storm's cumman, John.'.*

Cummerlan *SW* Cumberland.

Curly kue a flourish or bold stroke in writing, etc.

Curly powe a curled poll or head of hair. *'Dainty Davie, curly powe.'.*

Cursen christen.

Cursenmas, Cursmas Christmas. *'At Cursmas mery may ye dance.'.*

Cussin cousin.

Custa *C* comest thou? *'Gwordy, whoar custa frae?'.*

Cute acute, clever. *'He's nit sea 'cute to wussel oor Jack.'.*

Cuthbert an ass or donkey; idiot or simpleton.

Cuz comes. *'He cuz ower to see us now and than.'.*

Cuze accuse.

Cwol *C, N, E* coal.

Cwoorse *C, N, E* coarse, course.

Cwoort *C, NE* court.

Daar *C, E* dare. **Daarent** *C, E* dare not.

Daarentwatter Derwentwater.

Dab an expert one.

Daddle to walk or work slowly; to trifle; the hand. *'And give us a shak o'thy daddle.'.*

Daddy long-legs the *Tipula* or long-legs insect. (see Jenny spinner).

Dade, Dady *N* dada, daddy, father.

Daffan' joking, bantering.

Daffy *C* the daffodil.

Daffy-doon-dilly *C* the daffodil. *Pseudo-narcissus. 'Willy Wurdswuth reatt a grand poem aboot daffy-doon-dillys.'.*

Daft silly, wanton. *'Oor Jack's fairly daft about her.'*; idiotic. *'He's nobbut daftish.' 'Ey, daft as a besom.'.*

Dancin' mad in a towering or high passion.

Dander passion, excitement; a blow. *'His dander's up.'.*

Dansen *C* dancing.

Dar *C* dare.

Darkan' lurking; listening without appearing to do so.

Darken *C* to stand or be in the way. *'She sal niver darken my door na mair.'.*

Darknin' evening twilight.

Darna *N* dare not.

Darter *C* quick person.

Daur *N* dare.

Dawted *C* doted, foolish.

Dawwn *SW* down. *'Let's ga dawwn to t'shooar an' hev a dook.'.*

Dawwt *SW* doubt.

Dawwter *SW* daughter.

Daycent *SW* decent, worthy, favourable. *'A varra daycent man.' 'A daycent swort of a day.'.*

Dea *C* do.

Deamm *C, SW* dame; mistress of the house; wife.

Deddy *C* dada, daddy, father.

Dee die; do.

Dee *N, E* do. *'Will ta ivver dee it agyan.'.*

Deead *SW* dead.

Deeaf *SW* deaf.

Deean' *C* doing.

Deeath *SW* death.

Deeav *SW* to deafen; to stun with noise.

Deed *B* indeed; correct. **Deed** *C, N, E* dead.

Deef *C, N, E* deaf.

Deel devil.

Deepness *C* depth.

Deer door.

Deeth *C, N, E* death.

Deeval *N, E,* **Deil** *N* devil.

Deeve *C, N* to deafen; to stun with noise.

Deft *C* quiet, silent. **Deft** *N* handy. *'Jonty's varra deft wid pleugh.'.*

Deg *C* to ooze; to flow gently and slowly like a moist ulcer or *'deggan sare.'.*

Dench *C* squeamish; delicate; to drench.

Despart *C* desperate; inveterate; great. *'He's a despart fellow for drinkin'.'.*

Deuh *C, E* do. **Deun** done. **Deun out** *C* fatigued. *'Yer mam's deun out wid hoose wark.'.* **Deun ower** done over. *'Yer fadder's deun ower wid ale.'.*

Deur door, *'Steukk that deur, lass.'.*

Dewe *SW* do, dew; (pronounced day-oo, quickly).

Deyke *N* hedge.

Dicky not good; he's ruined, or dead. *'It's dicky wid him.'.*

Difficulter *C* more difficult.

Dig dog. *'Yer brudder's digs will feight yananudder.'.*

Dilly dally *C* to waste time; flighty. *'Yer Tilly nobbet a dilly dally lass.'.*

Din noise.

Dinna, Dinnet *C* do not.

Dint *E* to indent or dent; vigour; energy; thrift. *'He hez some dint in him'* - he will make his mark.

Dintless *E* lacking in energy.

Dis does. **Dis ta** does thou, do you. *"Dis ta think that's t'reet yan ta sell.'.*

Dish feaast hollow-faced; feminine.

Dish't defeated, overcome.

Disjest *C, E* digest.

Dispart *N* desperate; inveterate; great. *'He's a dispart fellow for drinkin'.'.*

Dissenton *C* Distington.

Dista *G, not E* see Dis Ta.

Div *B, N, E* do. *'Div ye gang to Wigton market?'.* **Divent** do not. **Diverna** *C* do not. **Divvent** do not. *'Now, divvent liken me to hur.'.* **Divvern't** *W* do not.

Divval *C, E, SW* devil.

Divval 'munt *C* mischievous, mischief-making. *'Dinna fret lass, yer fadder diz it for divval 'munt.'.*

Dix, Diz *N, E* does.

Dizzen *N, E* dozen; to bedeck or adorn, to decorate.

Do thee *C* a command. *'Do thee gang to thy wark.'.*

Dobbin *B* an old horse.

Doff to take off; to undress.

Dog cheap very cheap; much within its value.

Dog fo' an undecided fall in wrestling; a draw, the advantages being equal.

Dog trail a hound race or trail.

Dogger't *C* beggared, reduced to extreme poverty.

Dollop *C* a lump; a large share.

Dolly an instrument to twirl or agitate clothes within the wash-tub. **Dolly tub** the tub where clothes were once washed.

Don to do on; to dress.

Done out *C* fatigued.

Donky dank, damp, moist, humid or wet. **Donky weather** *C* mist and rain. *'It's a donky day, Dick.'....'Ey, rayder slattery.'*

Doo *C* a gathering, feast or merry making; something exciting. *'We'd a grand doo tudder neet wid yer mudder.'.*

Dooer *C, E* door. **Dooer steann** the threshold, door step.

Dook to bathe or swim; to duck; to dive. **Dookers** a male swimming costume or swimming trunks.

Doon *C, N, E* down; done. **Doon fo'** done for; the low parts around mountains where sheep shelter in bad weather; a fall of rain. **Doon't** knocked down; felled. *'Dick doon't him at t'furst bat.'.*

Doonbank *C, N* downwards.

Doose *C, N* a slap. *'Aa'll doose thy chops.'*; jolly, hospitable, open-handed; having a good appearance.

Doot *C, N, E* doubt. **Dootsam** *C, N* doubtful.

Dopy *C* a dope, simpleton or fool.

Dost does.

Dowdy slovenly, disorderly; negligent; not of neat appear-ance.

Dowter daughter. *'Ma new la'al dowters call't Emilly.'*.

Draa *SW* draw; to catch or overtake. *'He's off, bit we'll seunn draa him.'*.

Drabble draggle or make wet and dirty.

Draik't wet. **Drayk't, Dreak't** *N*, **Dreeav't** *SW*, **Dreuv't** *C* saturated with water,

Dreav *C, N, E* drove, did drive.

Dreeam dream.

Dreed *C, NE* dread. *'He niver dreedit sec a thing.'*.

Dreesom' *N* tiresome, lengthy.

Dreuv *C, N* drove; did drive.

Dreyve *NW* drive.

Driddle *C* a corruption of dribble; to fall in small drops or slow running; to slaver as a child or idiot.

Dridge dredge; to sprinkle.

Driss *C* dress.

Drisser dresser - a table or bench where meat and other foods are dressed or prepared; the crockery shelf.

Dro' *C, E* draw.

Drook't *C* severely wet. *'Issac gat drook't in t'beck.'*.

Drooken drunken.

Droon drown.

Drooty, Drufty droughty (weather).

Drouth *C, B, N* thirst.

Droven *C, E* driven.

Drucken, Drukken drunken.

Druss *N* dress.

Druv *C, N* drove; did drive. **Druvven** *C, E* driven.

Dryish *C, SW* thirsty; fine weather.

Du do; a gathering, feast or merry making; something exciting. **Duan** *SW* doing.

Dubersom' *C* dubious; in some doubt.

Dud did. *'Dud ta nivver see her ageann efter t'tansy.'*. **Dudn't, Dud n't** did not. *'I dudn't see yer at t'fair, as i dudn't ga.'*. **Dud ta?** didst thou?.

Duer *SW* door.

Dulbert *C*, **Dullbert** *E* a dull individual, stupid, blockish, slow of understanding etc.

Dum dumb.

Dumpy *C* short and thick. *'La'al Mary's a dumpy wee lass, if ivver I saw yan.'*.

Dun *C* done. **Dun ower** *C* done over; tired or finished. **Dunnet** do not.

Dunder heed a blockhead, stupid fellow or person deficient in understanding..

Dunnecan *E* a privy or toilet.

Dunsh to butt with elbow or knee.

Durs n't durst not or dare not.

Durt dirt. **Durtment** anything valueless or despicable.

Dus does. *'Mind thoo nivver dus agean.'*. **Dust ta, Dusta** does thou, do you. *'What dusta think?'*.

Dust uproar, disturbance. *'Kick up a dust.'*

Dwoat, Dwoted *C, E* doted, foolish.

Dyke *C, SW* hedge.

E *C* the eye; I.

E *SW* in. *'He'll rin or feyt ivver a yan e' aa Cummerlan.'*.

E'bn even.

E'e eye.

Earan errand; task to perform.

Eb'm even; one of bad character or habits - *'a bad eb'm.'.*

Eb'm endways even endwise, continuous, without interruption. *'He mendi't eb'm endways.'.*

Eb'n, **Ebn** even.

Eeast *SW* east.

Eeat *SW* eat.

Eeb'nin', Eebnin evening.

Een eyes.

Eernin *SW* earning.

Efter after. *'Meet me up t'lonnin efter t'fair.'.* **Efter a bit** after a while.

Efter-neun, **Efterneun** afternoon. *'Gud efterneun ivrybody.'.*

Efterword afterward; a word or expression habitually repeated.

Eg on *C* to urge and encourage. *'Dunnet eg on oald Sam to sing ageun.'.*

Elba elbow. **Elba' grease** hard rubbing or polishing; using hands and elbows.

Elebben eleven.

En *SW* than. *'I's gittan mair en I want.'.*

En' *N* end.

End part. *'A girt end of its for t'oald lass.';* to set upright. *'End him up, lads, were off heamm';* the river Ehen was once often pronounced 'end'.

Eneuf *C* enough.

Enny *C, E* any. *'Thay refuse't ta let oald Jwon hev enny mair yal.'.* **Enny way** *C* every way. *'This is enny way as good as oor weddin day.'.*

Er *G, not E* are. *'Ho er ye to-day, bonny lass?'.*

Er *NW* nor.

Ern *NE* iron.

Est *N, E* nest.

Et *C* at.

Et *C, SW* to. *'Gang et thresh.'.* (common in the 18th century).

Eustat' *SW* Easthwaite in Netherwasdale, *'thwaite'* is thus shortened in some instances, but not in all cases.

Ex *SW* ask.

Expect *C* to suppose. *'I expect it's reet.'.*

Ey yes, aye.

Eyce *NW, SW* ice.

Eydle *NW, SW* idle.

Eye *C* yes. *'Eye, I's gaan to Workiton for a par o'new shun.'.*

Ez *C* as.

Faa *N, SW* fall; a turn or bout of wrestling.

Faal *N*, **Faald** *SW* fold.

Faallen wrang *N* become pregnant.

Faan *N, SW* fallen; slaken as lime.

Faat *SW* fault.

Fadder *C, E, SW* father. *'Fadder, carf t'beef at t'teabbel.'.*

Faff to mess about or waste time; to work ineffectively. *'Stop faffin abeutt.'.* **Faffle** *C* to trifle; imperfect fallow. **Fafflement** *C* trifling and unnecessary work.

Fag fatigue, *'Fadder was sair fag't efter wark';* to hang back.

Fag end the worthless remains; the last.

Faggit *N*, **Faggot** a term of contempt or reproach. *'An oald faggot!'.*

Fairish tolerably good or moderately satisfactory.

Fallopy, **Fally like** *C* untidy.

Famish famous; notable, *'Wudswurth*

was a famish poet fray Cockermuth.'. **Famish'd** hungry or starving

Fan *N,* **Fand** *C, E* found.

Far away by much; by far. *'This is far away better than last neet.'.*

Far the weel *C,* **Fares taw eel** *N, E* farewell. *'Fares taw eel fayther! am off to Workiton.'.*

Farder farther or further. **Fardest** farthest.

Fash trouble; inconvenience; to get annoyed or exasperated. *'I'll nivver be fash't any mair wid it.'.* **Fashious** become annoying or troublesome through intoxication.

Fassen *C, E* fasten.

Fause *E, N* cunning, sly; artful; false.

Faver *C* family resemblance. *'He favers his fadder mair than t'others.'.*

Faver *C, N,* **Favver** *SW* fever.

Fawwnd *C, E, SW* found.

Faymish famous.

Fayther *N* father. *'Oor Fayther forgat t'oald lass's burthday.'.*

Feale *N* fail.

Fearfo' *N,* **Fearful** *C, SW* extraordinary. *'They're fearfo' kind fray Kiprangill.'.*

Feass face; assurance or boldness. *'He hez a feass for ought.*

Feckless feeble, unsub-stantial.

Fedder *C, N, E* feather.

Feeast *SW* feast.

Feeaver *SW* fever.

Feek *C* to be uneasy or anxious. *'In a feek.'.*

Feel *N* smooth.

Feels *N* fields.

Feg *C* fig; not a care, contemptuous, *'He duzzent care a feg.'.*

Feght *N,* **Feight** fight. *'Oor digs will nivver feight yan anudder.'.*

Fek *C* eke, enlarge or lengthen, to prolong; to help or aid.

Fell in wid *C, SW* met with by chance; joined a gang or group.

Felt felled; thrown or cut down.

Fettle *B* to beat. *'Aa'l fettle his lug for am.'.*

Fettle to fit; put in order; health or condition. *'What fettle's thy fadder in today?'.*

Feull *C, N, E* fool.

Feutt *C* foot, speed, pace. *'He went a parlish feutt ower t'moor.'.* **Feutt bo** *C* the game of football; *'Uppies and Downies'* played in Workington every Easter.

Fewsom' shapely, becoming.

Feyne *B* fine, good, handsome, not a problem. *'Jack's a fine laal lad in skeul.'.* **Feyne** *N, NW* a term of comparison; as, *'a feyne girt an.' ....'a feyne laal an.'.*

Feyt *C, E, SW* fight. **Feytin** *C* fighting.

Fidgetty uneasy, impatient.

Fiffle-fafflement *C* trifling and unnecessary work.

Fift fifth. **Filthment** dirt; anything inferior or offensive; low characters.

Finely *C, SW* healthy. *'I's finely, and fadder's finely an'o'.'.*

Finnd find.

Fir't *C* fired. *'He fir't his gun at the cro.'.*

Firtle *C* to trifle and appear busy.

Fit disposed. **Fit** *N* foot, speed, pace. *'He went a parlish fit ower t'moor.'*; fought.

Flacks *C* flakes. *'A strinkle of sna*

flacks all ower t'yard.'.

Flaggen *C* slowing down or labouring. *'T'oald horse seemed ta be flaggen a bit.'*.

Flaitch *C* to flatter; a flatterer.

Flak *C* tired or exhausted, liable to go to sleep. *'T'oald lass just flak'd out by t'ingle.'*.

Flakker *C* to laugh heartily as a child does; to flapper.

Flam to carjole, flatter grossly, blarney; falsehood told jestingly, not in earnest.

Flang did fling; having flung.

Flap *E* a rude and boisterous girl (or hoyden); to wander or work without a purpose; agitated or disturbed, *'She's just flappan' up and down an' o'about nought.'*. **Flapper't** *C* nervous, frightened.

Flate afraid.

Flay to frighten. **Flaysom'** frightful. **Flayt** frightened. **Flaytly** timidly.

Flear, Fleear *C, N, SW,* **Fleer** *C, B, N* the floor. *'Oor lass has wesh'd the parlour fleer.'*. **Fleer't** *B* floored, *'Willy fleer't him in t'ring'* - threw him down on the floor at wrestling. **Fleur** floor.

Flee fly. **Fleean** flying. **Fleet** *C, SW.* flight. **Fleet** *N* to flee or remove, and especially when in debt. *'They mead a moonleet fleet on 't.'*. **Fleght** *N* flight.

Fleet *C* the lot; the whole number or quantity. *'Thou's can't t'heall fleet o'them.'*.

Fleud, Fleudd flood.

Fleukk *B* feather.

Fleuterment ridiculous talk.

Fliar to laugh heartily; to laugh and talk loudly.

Flinders *C* fragments; broken pieces. *'I'll knock tha o'to flinders.'*.

Flit *C, N* flight; to flee or remove, especially when in debt. *'They mead a moonleet flit on 't.'*.

Flooar flower; flour.

Fluer *SW* floor.

Fluet *C* a stroke. *'Hit him a fluet ower t'lug.'*.

Flummery flattering abundance of words (verbiage or verbosity).

Flung deceived; defeated. *'He was fairly flung.'*.

Flyte *N* to jeer; scold.

Fo fall; a turn or bout of wrestling. **Fo' out** fall out, to quarrel. **Fo'through** *C* When a arrangement, deal or project fails it is said to fall through. *'Sellin t'farm as fo'through.'*. **Fo-en** *C* fallen, slaken.

Foak *C* folk.

Foald *C* fold. *'Side t'teabbel an' foald up t'cleath.'*.

Foat fault.

Foisty having a musty scent.

Fole *N* fold.

Foll'et followed.

Foo *N* drunk; to fill. *'Foo that cup.'*.

Fooal *SW* fool.

Fooat *SW* foot, speed, pace. *'He went a parlish fooat ower t'moor.'*.

Foond *C* to purpose; intend. *'I foond to build a house.' (nearly obsolete in 1878)*.

Foor *C* front *'T'foor door's pent't rid.'*. **Foor-hand** beforehand. **Foorberin** *C* fore-warning. **Foormest** foremost. **Foorseet** foresight. **Foorsett** to anticipate; to way-lay.

Foothy *C* bulky, hospitable; *N, E* kind, liberal.

Footstart head start or to start before the rest.

For going. *'Whoar is ta for to-day?'...'I's for Whitten.'*. **For bye** *N* besides; over and above. **For o'** *G* although, notwith-standing.

For-gat, **For-git** forgot, forget. **For-ivver** forever; very much or many. *'Theer was for-ivver o'fwok at t'fair.'*. **For-nenst** *C, N* opposite to. *'Their hoose is eb'n for-nenst ours.'*.

For-ther *N* farther, further; to forward or promote. **Forder** *C* to forward; to assist; to promote. **Fore-bears** *N* ancestors. **Forgat, Forgit** forget.

Formable *C* properly arranged; in due form.

Fornenst *NE* opposite to: over against. (see Anenst.)

Forra *SW* forward, straight. **Forrad** *SW* forward. **Forrat** *C, N, E* forward, straight. **Forseakk** forsake.

Fortneth *C, E* fortnight.

Fote *C, E* fault.

Fourt fourth.

Fower four.

Fowt fought.

Foxy *B* crafty, sly or cunningly.

Fratch a quarrel or disagreement; a noisy quarrel. *'He aye snapt his thooms for a bit of a fratch'*. **Fratchy** argumentative. **Frath'an** *C, N* quarrelling.

Fray from.

Fred *E, SW* freed; cleared out.

Freeght *N* fright.

Freen, Freend *N* friend.

Freet *C, E, SW* fright; fret. **Freet** *N* to grieve; to tear. **Freeten** frighten.

Freh *N* from.

Fren *C* friend.

Fret *C* to grieve; to tear.

Frev *C, N, SW* from. **Frey** *N, NW* from.

Frind *C, N, E* friend.

Frizzle fry or roast.

Froff *C*, **Frough** *N* easily broken. *'Frough as a carrot.'*.

Frowe a fat and morose woman. **Frowsy** *B* an overgrown woman.

Frudge *N* to press; to brush past or against in a rude manner.

Fudderson' *C* troublesome; annoying.

Fuffy *N* very light and loose.

Fummel a blundering attempt; a fumble.

Fun *N*, **Fund** *C, E* found.

Furst first. **Furst feutt** *N* the person who first enters the house on New Year's day.

Futterson' *C* troublesome; annoying.

Fwok folk. The men say *'woman fwok'* and *'woman body.'* The woman say *'men fwok '* and *'man body.'*.

Fwoor for.

Fwoorarm forearm.

Fwoorneun forenoon.

Fwoorseet foresight.

Fwoorsuer *C* foreshore.

Fwoortelt *C* foretold.

Fwoortin *C* fourteen.

Fwoortun *C* fortune.

Fwor'ge *C* forgive. *'He'll nivver fwor'ge yer.'*.

Fworce force; a waterfall as *Scale Force* etc.

Fwore for.

Fwore-elders ancestors.

Fwore-hand beforehand.

Fworeivver *C* forever.

Fworemest foremost.

Fworivver forever.

Fworsuer *C* for sure; a certainty.

Ga *C, SW.* go. **Gaan** going.

Ga'me *C* gave me.

Gab the mouth; idle talk. *'Mary gabs on fworeivver an' tells yer nowt.'.* **Gabble** to talk quickly and not wisely.

Gadgee person (usually male) *'Look at yon gadgee fra Wigton.'.*

Gaffer *C* governor or foreman; master. Thought to have been introduced with the railways.

Gah *C* go. *'I's gah t'toon this efterneun.'.*

Gam *NW, E* game.

Gammel gamble.

Gammy *N* sore; lame.

Gan *N* go.

Gang *B* turn to play or go. *'Its thy gang noo.'.* **Gang** go. **Gangan** going. **Gangin's on** proceedings, events. *'Ey, theer was fine gangin's on at t'weddin'.'.* **Gangs** *C, E, SW* goes, *'He gangs out iv'ry neet to t'inn.'.* **Gans** *N* goes, *'He gans iv'ry day to see t'oald lass at yem.'.*

Gar to compel. *'A'll gar tha gang.'.*

Garrak *C* awkward. *'As garrak as a unbroken cowt.'.*

Garron *C* a tall and awkward horse.

Garron *N* anything high or tall and ungainly.

Gas *C* goes.

Gat got. *'Our taty tops gat a snapin' wi'frost.'.*

Gawky *N* a staring idiotical person; awkward; ungainly.

Gawwn *SW.* gown or dress.

Gaz *C, N, SW* goes. *'She nivver gaz to see yer mam.'.*

Ge give. *'Ge me that.'.* **Ge'en** given. *'He's ge'en tul't'- he is disposed to it.*

Gean, Geann *C, N, E* gone.

Geatt gate; path; way. *'Git out o'my geatt.'.*

Gedder gather.

Gee *C* offence, *'He's teaun t'gee.'.*

Gee give. *'Gee me that.'.*

Gee's *N* gives; give us.

Gees *N* gives; give me.

Geh *N* gave. *'He geh t'hoose to mither, when t'berry'd fayther.'.*

Gether gather.

Geud, Geudd *N* good.

Gev *C* give. *'She gev a knattle on t'flags wid her heel.'.* **Gev** *C, E, SW* gave. *'He gev sek a shout!'.*

Geyde *NW, SW* guide.

Gez *SW* goes. *'He gez wid her to church iv'ry sunday.'.*

Ghem *C* game.

Gi 'them 't, Gi'tha, Gi'the 't give thou it; give thee, give thee it, give it to them.

Gidder gather.

Gif *N* if.

Gin given. *'He's gin yer hoose t'lad.*

Gin *N* if. *'Gin ye'll gan I'll gan.'.*

Ginnel lane or narrow passage.

Girdle a circular iron baking plate.

Girn *C* grin or pull a face.

Girse *C, SW* grass, *'Theer laal girse in our girsin' field t'year.'.*

Girt *C* great; friendly. **Girt** *NE* great.

Git get; offspring. *'They're o'his oan*

git.'. **Git it** *C* get it; receive it. **Git shot** *C* get rid of; dispose of. *'They wantit to git shot on him.'.* **Git'n** got, gotten, *'He's git'n his crowdy.'.* **Gittan** *G, not E* getting. *'He's gittan it iv'ry whoar.'.* **Gitten** got, gotten.

Give ower stop or leave off. *'Is 't gaan to give ower sno'an think ye?'.*

Giz *C, E, SW* gives; give us or me.

Gleb, Gleg *N* sharp, quick. *'He's gleg at that job.';* working smoothly.

Glenderan' *C* looking earnestly.

Glent *C,* **Glint** *N* glance.

Gleym *N,* to look sidewise.

Gloer *C, SW,* **Gloor** *N* to stare.

Glop *C, SW* to stare; to look wildly.

Glower *N* to stare or glare.

Glowt *SW* a clumsy fellow.

Glwore *C, SW* to stare.

Gob *C, N* mouth. *'Shut yer gob, or I'll shut in fwor yer.';* idle talk; to spit.

Goller *C, N* to shout; to bark or talk loudly.

Good eb'n good evening.

Goodin' *B* indulging. *'Yer faythers goodin' his sel.'*.

Goon *C, N, E* gown or dress.

Goose gogs gooseberries.

Gowe *C* go.

Gowk a fool; the core. *'It's badly burnt lime - it's nought bit gowks.'.*

Gran *N* grand, *'Yer granfadder's varra old.'.* **Granfadder** grandfather.

Granky *E* crotchety; sickly or unwell and complaining, *'Nobbet varry granky.'* (see Cranky).

Grape *N* grope, feel. **Grapple** *C* to wrestle.

Grawe *C, E* grow.

Grayseunn *C* Greysouthen village and township - anciently *Crakesothen.*

Gree agree. *'They're about 'greeax for a horse.'.*

Greeat *SW,* **Greet** great; greet; friendly.

Grend *SW* ground, grind.

Greymy *N* grimy or begrimed; soiled or dusty; sooty.

Grin *N* ground, grind.

Growan growing; grown. *'H's growan int' a reet pleesant la'al lad.'.* **Growe** *C, E* grow.

Grumfy *C* grumpy orcomplaining, ailing or believing to be so.

Grummel grumble.

Grun *N,* **Grund** *C, E* ground, grind.

Gud *C* good.

Gumption sense or shrewdness. *'He's nivver gat the gumption to see it's 'rang.'.*

Gurn *C, N* grin or pull a face. *'Give ower gurnin' lass or thou'll git it.'.* (see Set a feass).

Gurse *N* grass.

Gurt *C, N* great; friendly.

Gwordy *C* the name George; people from the North East of England (Geordies).

Gworge *N* the name George.

H'ard heard. *'He niver h'ard tell on't.'.*

Ha-way *SW* go along; come on.

Haa *N, NE, SW* hall.

Haald *SW* hold; shelter. *'T' hev and t' haald.'.*

Hae *C* hare; hair.

Haf *N,* **Hafe** half.

Haffle *N* to be undecided.

Hairly *N* hardly; scarcely.

Hakes *C* doings, happenings or events. *'Sek hakes at t'fair last* *neet!'.*

Hakker *C* to stammer. *'He hakkers an'gits nin on wid his talk.'.*

Hale *C* to do effectively, forcibly; to drive the ball to the winning-post. *'T'Uppies haled the ball at Workiton t'year.'.*

Ham sam *C* promiscuous; all in confusion.

Han' hand.

Hand direction. *'He's gone toward Ireby and that hand.'.*

Hank efter *C* a wish, longing or desire. (see Hankeran').

Hankeran *C, E, N* a wish, longing or desire. *'He still hez a hankeran' for yer lass Jonty.'.*

Hanklin *C, E, N* a wish, longing or desire. (see Hankeran').

Hannel handle; a large pail or bucket.

Hap to cover. *'She hap't o't'barns at bed-time.*

Hap'm *C* happen. *'Hap'm I see thee in t'mwornin'.'.*

Hard *C* hardy. *'He's as hard as a fell teadd.'*; turning sour - said of beer, etc.

Hard heard. *'I hard whiff of thy news last neet.'.* **Hard tell** heard of. *'I nivver hard tell o'see a thing.'.*

Hardfully *C* industriously. *'Bob gits his leevin reet hardfully.'.*

Harp on complain excessively and repeatedly; to often refer to an unpleasant subject or event.

Harrish harass. **Harrishin'** *N* violent invasion; harrying.

Hash *C* harsh.

Hat did hit.

Hawws, Hawwse *SW* house.

Hay hey, often spoken to grab someones attention; what did you say?.

Hay *N* have. *'I hay'the noo.'- I comprehend.*

Hayness *C* heinous - great, monstrous, extraordinary etc. *'Hayness fine.'* or *'Hayness dirty.'.*

Headd hid.

Heal, Heall whole. *'Now giz us t'heall story, nut just yer side of gangin's on.'.*

Heam, Heamm home. **Heamly, Heammly** homely. **Heamm comin'** returning. *'I whope thou'll hev a hearty heamm comin'.'.*

Hear, Hearr hair; hare.

Heasst haste.

Heast *C, E* haste; hasten.

Heat, Heatt hot; rather hot.

Hed had. **Hed n't, Hedn't** *C* had not

Hee *C, N, E* high.

Heead *SW,* **Heed** *C, N* head.

Heeap *SW* heap, a good many. *'Heeaps o'things.'.*

Heeard heard. *'I heeard about yer weddin' fray t'curate.'.*

Heed-yak *SW,* **Heed-yik** *N,* **Heedwark** *C* headache.

Heedstan' headstone, a memorial or gravestone.

Heemest highest.

Heemm *C, SW* home, *'Expect we'll soon git heamm to bed.'.*

Heet height.

Heid *C, SW* head.

Helpsom' *C* ready and willing to help. *'Oor Mary's nut varra help-som.'.*

Hemmer *N* hammer.

Hennet *N* have not.

Hereabouts *C,* **Hereaway** in this neighbourhood.

Hes has. **Hes ta** has thee or has thou?, have you? *'Hes ta come fray yer teas.'.*

Het hot; rather hot; to heat; heated.

Het feutt *C, SW* in a great hurry. *'He's het feutt'd it ower theer to see her.'.*

Het trod *N* in close pursuit. *'He follow't the reivers on the het trod.'.*

Hettish hot; rather hot.

Heud, Heudd hid.

Hev have. *'I hev'the noo.'*- I comprehend. **Hev at** to set to or begin a task. **Hevvent** have not.

Hey *C, SW* high.

Heyde *N* hide; to beat.

Hez has, hath *'He hez tha noo'*- he is thy master.

Hide *C, E, SW* hide; to beat.

Hilth health.

Himsel' himself.

Hin en' *N* hinder, opposite or back end.

Hing hang. *'Hing on Jack, lets gaa heamm by the beck.'.* **Hing on** hang or hold on; wait or hold up; continue; stick to it.

His-sel himself.

Hit on to agree *'They don't hit on about it.'.*

Hitten hit.

Hiz *N* us. **Hizzy** *N* huzzy, a housewife's pocket case for needles and thread; hussy.

Ho how, *'Ho er ye to-day, bonny lass?'.*

Ho *C* hall.

Ho-way *C* go along; come on.

Hoaf *C* half. **Hoaflins** half-done; half-witted; half-shares.

Hoald *C, E* to hold; shelter. *'They've nowder house nor hoald to draw teah.'.*

Hod to hold; shelter. *'Keep hod of t'beukk, till Setterday neet.'.* **Hod bye** stand out of the way.

Hod te watter be silent; shut up and keep quiet. *'Hod te watter lass, dunnet tell iv'ry yan.'.*

Hodden *C* held. *'Lampla' club's still hodden o't second Friday o'Joon.'.*

Hoddit *C, E* hold it; held. *'Hoddit and dunnet let it gaa.'.*

Hofe half. *'Hofe a shillin' is a tanner.'.*

Hofe thick *C* a foolish person; a half-fatted animal.

Hoo how, *'Hoo ur ye?'.*

Hoo-way *C* go along; come on. *'Hoo-way! I'll nut stop here forivver.'.*

Hooas *SW* house.

Hooivver *C* however.

Hoon *N,* **Hoond** *C, E* hound. *'Jwon Peel an' his hoond's come fray Coadbeck.'.*

Hoose *C, N* house.

Hote halt; limp in walk..

Howdy *N* midwife.

Howe *C* a hoe; hollow, empty; a gentle hill or eminence, or knoll; spoken to a cow it means - *'go'.*

Howe neet *E* the silence of the dead of night.

Howk to dig; to scratch in the earth etc; to punish.

Howker *C* a large one.

Hubble *C* a crowd. *'A hubble o'fwok at church for t'berryin'.'.*

Hudden *C, N, E* hidden.

Hulk *C* a tall, lazy fellow. *'A girt lang hulk.'.*

Hun *N* to hound; a hound. *'Jwon*

Peel's huns are out on yon fell.'.

Hup up. *'Hup wi' tha' git out o'yer bed.'.*

Hur her.

Hurd herd; heard.

Huz *C, SW* us. *'Ham an' eggs fwoor huz teas.'.*

Hysta *C* hi thee.

I' a contraction of *'I'* or *'in'*.

I's I am. *'I's to hev her.'*

Ib-nin', Ibnin evening.

Ider either.

Ilk, Ilka *N* each; every.

Ill to degrade or slander. *'Don't ill a body if you can't say weel o'yan.'*; bad or evil. (see Ill teull).

Ill turn an injury or sickness.

Ill farrant *N* ill-favoured.

Imma in me.

Immead'tly *SW* immediately.

In friendly; accepted by others. *'He gat in wi't'oald fwok, and he keeps in.'.*

In a twitter *N* soon, quickly.

In anonder under; beneath.

In roads to progress with a task. *'Oor lass is makin' in roads with the cleeanin'.'.*

Inam, Inman in him.

Inklin' a slight hint or intimation; a thought or feeling. *'Jack hed an inklin' he was reet efter all.'.*

Insteed *N* instead.

Inteutt, Intil't *N E* into it.

Intul *C* in too. *'He coonted t'money intul my fist.'*; **Intul't** *C* into it.

Ir are, *'Ir ye gaan away?'.*

Irrant are not.

Is are, *'Hey Jonty, how is ye to-day?'.*

Ish a ending often added to other words, may suggest a degree of uncertainty. eg. *goodish, badish,, fairish, hee-ish up, far-ish away.*

Ister is there. *'Ister enny churry ceakk fwoor the vicar?'.*

Ither *N* other.

Ittal It'll or it will, *'Ittall hev to do, theer's nin left!'.*

Iv *C, N* in. *'He's lishest lad iv o'Brumfell parish.'.*

Iv'ry *C* every.

Iv'ry like every now and then.

Iv'ry whoar *C,* **Iv'rything** everything.

Ivry, Ivvery *C* every.

Ivver ever. **Ivverly** *E* frequently; contin-uously.

Ize I is. *I am.*

Jam to squeeze. *'T'lads and lasses war all jam'd up in yan la'al car.'*; to press against; to wedge.

Jamp jumped, leapt.

Jant *C* an outing, pleasure trip or jaunt. *'I's been on oaldfwoks church jant to Seaskeall.'.*

Jaw *C* bad language.

Jedder *C* to shake; to jar; discord.

Jeelas *N, E* jealous.

Jert *C, SW* jerk; to pitch a stone with the hand from the hip.

Jew't cheated.

Jimp tight; too little.

Job an event. *'It's a bad job for us o'.'.*

Joggle *C* to push; to disturb the elbow of a person writing.

Jook *C* a long and tiresome journey on foot

Joon *C* June.

Joop't *B* to be domineered over by a woman.

Jope to splash; to bespatter. (see Slopper).

Jopins anything spilled..

Jordy *N, NW* the name George;

Geordies, the people from the North East of England.

Jowat *NW* a term of effeminacy. *'He's a feckless jowat.'.*

Jowl *C* the jaw; to jumble; This word often relates more particularly to the disturbing of a vessel containing fluid.

Jull *C* to shake; to jar; discord.

Jum wid *C* to fall in with; to meet accidentally.

Jummel jumble.

Jurnal *C* journal, diary or record book.

Just now shortly, soon. *'I'll come just now.'.*

Jwoke joke.

Jwon *C* John. *'D'ye ken Jwon Peel.'.*

Jworam *N* a large mess; abundance.

Ka bye stand out of the way; come by.

Kack hand'd left handed. *'Yan of ma dowters kack hand'd.'*; clumsy when performing a task using the hands.

Kay key. *'I seen him throo t'kaywholl.'.*

Keah *SW* key.

Keak *C, N, E* cake.

Keall kale; greens; porridge of oatmeal.

Keam *N, E,* **Keamm** *NE* comb.

Kear, Kearr *C* care.

Keas case.

Keb feuttit *E* a person who walks with the toes turned inward.

Keckle *C, E, SW* cackle, laugh.

Keeak *SW* cake.

Keen on fond of. *'Yer chap's keen on yer fadder's churry ceakk.'.*

Keep't kept.

Kelk *C* to hit roughly; a severe blow. *'An ugly kelk.'.*

Kelker *C* a heavy blow. **Kelkin'** *C* a beating.

Kelter *C* money, riches.

Ken to know; to see; to remember. **Kennin'** knowing. *'That youngster's growan'out o'kennin'.'.*

Kersen to christen. *'Efter t'weddin, we'll hev t'kersenin'.'.*

Kersenmas, Kersmas Christmas. *'At Kersenmas mery may ye dance.'.*

Kessen cast. *'T'sky's ower-kessen.'.* **Kessen metal** *C* cast iron.

Kessick *C* Keswick.

Kest cast. *'T'Beerpot warks ner Workiton maks owt fray kest metal.'.*

Keuk cook.

Keul, Keull cool.

Keyn', Keynd *NW* kind.

Keyte *N* the belly.

Kill't killed.

Kill't t'crack stopped a conversation by adding an irrelevant or foolish remark, generally out of context.

Kinnel kindle, ignite. **Kinnellin'** *C* materials to light a fire with.

Kipple *B* couple, *'They mak a fine kipple.'*; Two rams chained together by their horns are *kippl't*.

Kirk a church.

Kirk garth churchyard. **Kirk-gaan** church-going; regular in attendance at church.

Kist a chest.

Kites berries.

Kitlin *C* kitten.

Knaa *SW* know. **Knaanat** *SW* know not. *'I knaanat if t'berryin' ower yit.'.*

Knack *C, N, E* to talk quick, and attempt fine language. *'She knacks* *and talks like rotten sticks.'.*

Knack method. *'Dick hez t'knack to do iv'ry job.'.*

Knackered worn out; tired.

Knacks *C* nothing beyond ordinary or special. *'He's neah girt knacks.'.*

Kneaw, Kneaww *SW* knew.

Kneyf *NW* knife.

Knonnot *C, E* know not. *'I knonnot why he's gaan.'.*

Knur't *C* stunted; not freely grown.

Kurk a church.

Kursty Christopher.

Kyp't *C* bent. A saw is said to be *'kyp't'* when buckled or permanently bent or twisted.

Kyte *C, SW* the belly. *'T'Squires gat a greet kyte on him.'.*

Laa *N, SW* law; low.

La'al, Laal *C* little, or small *'Fray la'al acorns, greet oaks grawe.'.*

Laal house *C* a privy or outside toilet. (see Donnican).

Laan *N* land.

Labber *C* to splash in water.

Ladder lather.

Laddie *C, N* a lad. This word was applied to a person having a particular strong habit or propensity. *'He's a laddie for o'maks o'spwort.'.*

Laggin always behind; insulation to water tank or roofspace etc.

Laird *N* lord: landowner, yeoman.

Lam *E* to beat.

Lammin' *E* a thrashing.

Lampla' *C* Lamplugh.

Lan' *N* land.

Land *C* an estate in land. *'Willy Fisher o'Winscales hed three lands.'.* - or separate estates.

Land *C, SW* to arrive. *'He landit in yester neet.';* to receive; to find.

Lang long, tall, high. *'He'll be six feutt hee, and as good as he's lang.';* to long or wish for; along.

Lang end the final end.

Lang man *C, B* the middle finger.

Lang on *C* because of. *'It was o'lang o'him 'at I fell into t'beck.'.*

Lang sen *C, SW* long since.

Lang windit prolix; a long speech, argument or converstaion. *'Yer Mary's reet lang windit an' nivver shuts up.'.*

Langer longer.

Langer east shorter west *C* a deficiency in one part is compensated by abundance in another.

Langseyene *N* long since.

Langsom tedious. *'It's a langsom rwoad ower Hutton moor.'.*

Langsyne *N* long since.

Langways lengthwise. *'T'fleur's ten feútt langways an' six across.'.*

Lanky long and thin.

Lap *N* leapt.

Lap sidit *C* unequally balanced.

Larn learn - also to teach. *'He larns his scholars to read an' write.'.*

Larrop *C* to beat.

Lash out *C* to use a comb; to spend money, almost without a second thought, *'T'oald lass has lash'd out on a new dress.';* kick out or hit out.

Layt to seek. *'Gang an' layt t'kye heamm.'.*

Leaf, Leaff loaf. *'T'mudders mead a leaff of bread iv'ry day this week.'.*

Leann alone.

Leapp *C, SW* leapt.

Leastways at least or leastwise. *'It*

niver was seah, leastways I niver knew 't.'.

Leat, **Leatt** *C* late.

Leave gang, Leave hod let go; do not hold.

Leaydy *C, N, E* lady.

Leayk *N* play.

Leck to leak; a hard subsoil of clay and gravel.

Ledder to beat; leather.

Ledder lungs a garrulous or very talkative person. *'Oald ledder lungs nivver shuts up.'.*

Leddy *N* lady.

Ledge allege. *'He 'ledges it was still seah.'.*

Lee a lie; tell a lie.

Leeak *SW* look.

Leear liar.

Leeas *SW* lease.

Leeav *SW* leave.

Leeght light; to slight.

Leet light; window; to slight; to enlighten or explain; to alight etc. **Leeten** lighten. **Leetnin'** lightning.

Leet on *C* to meet with. *'I leet on him at t'cross rwoads past Rowrah.'.*

Leev, **Leeve** live. *'Ah furst com ta leeve here ten year since.'.* **Leevin** living. *'He's gitten a reet geud leevin fray prentin.'.* **Leevs** lives. *'He leevs someway out Cockermuth way.'.*

Leever sooner; rather. *'I'd leever hev this nor that'n.'.*

Legg it *C* run away. *'I telt the lad off and he legg'd it heamm.'.*

Leggan' away *C* walking quickly.

Len'me lend me. *'Wad ta len'me a shillin'?'.*

Let on speak; frequently used as *'Nivver let on'* - do not speakor tell, keep it secret.

Let'n let. *'He sud ha'let'n that aleann.'.*

Leugh *N* laugh or laughted.

Leuk *C, N, E,* **Leukk** *C, N* look.

Leukt *C* looked. *'Mattha was riddy fwor owt' at leukt like fun.'.*

Leuv *C, N, E,* **Leuvv** *N* love.

Leycence *N, NW* licence.

Leyfe *N, NW* life.

Leyke *N, NW* like.

Leykin' *N, NW* fondness; liking. *'Mey leykin' for thee I can't smudder.'*; a term of endear-ment to a child. *'Come hither, my leyl leykin'.'*.

Leykly *N* likely.

Leyl *B* small.

Leyle *N* little.

Liable reliable; apt; having a propensity to. *'He's liable to get drunk if he's ought in his pocket.'.*

Lift help or assistance. *'He'll give us a lift at a pinch.'.*

Lig to lie down.

Lig at lay to it; work at it vigorously. *'Lig at him, lad.'.*

Liggers *C* layers.

Liggin lying.

Likken *N, E* to compare; to match. *'Now, divvent liken me to hur.'.*

Likly *N* likely.

Lilly to flatter. *'She lilly 't t'cald man up till she gat him an' his money.'.*

Lines *C* banns of marriage. *'T' lines have gone in to t'parson.'.*

Lipe *E* a large portion, usually applied to land. *'T' railways teann a girt lipe off our croft.'.*

Lish *C, SW* supple; active.

Lissen *C* listen. *'Oald Jack was*

lissenan to the birds singan.'.

Livver *C, E* deliver.

Lo' *C, E* law; low.

Lob *C* to leap or run heavily; to throw usually in a under-arm fashion.

Lofe *C* offer; chance or opportunity *'He'd nea lofe o'selling.'.*; in some cases - head. *'Use yer lofe.'.*

Lonnin narrow lane or track, usually leading to an isolated field or dwelling.

Looance *C, E* allowance.

Lood loud.

Lopp't *C* chopped or cut. *'I's lopp't top off t' birk tree.'.*

Loppen leapt.

Lowp a leap or jump, either running or standing. The various kinds include Catskip, one hitch or hop and one jump. *'Yon lad's just lowp'd oor yer dyke.'.*

Lowse loose or loosen; out of service or apprenticeship. **Lowsely** loosely.

Lu-war lukewarm.

Lufter *C* abundance; a crowd, *'A heull lufter o' fwok co' frae Codebeck.'.*

Lugs ears.

Lump a dim, dull, and stupid character. *'He's nobbett a gurt lump.'.*

Lurry *C* hurry, *'Tak t'dog and lurry them sheep away.'.*

Lwoaf *C, N* loaf. *'T'mither beakk'd a lwoaf iv'ry day this week.'.*

Lwoase *C* to lose.

Lword *G, NW* lord. *'T'Curwins are lwords of t'manor at Workiton.*

Lwoze lose.

Ly ye! *N* listen ye!.

Lyle *SW* little.

Lysta! *C* listen.

Ma me.

Maa *N, SW* to cut with a scythe; to mow.

Maak *N, SW* make.

Maff, **Maffin** *C* a simple person.

Maffle to blunder; to mislead.

Mair *C, N, E* more, *'Ey's plenty mair where 'at came fray.'.*

Maist *N* most.

Maister *C, N, E* master, mister. *'Maister Dickinsun was browte up at Kiprangill.';* teacher, eg. *skooalmaister.*

Mak *C, E, SW* make.

Mak at *C* to attack. *'Oor bull mead at him full smack.'.*

Mak count on *C* to reckon on; to take into account.

Mak on *C* hurry on; to treat kindly; to encourage. *'Mak on him and he'll dea better.'.*

Mak out to progress. *'How is he makkan out wi'ma lass?'.*

Mak up till to seek favour. *'Mak up till her man.'.*

Makkan *C* making.

Maks types, kinds or sorts. *'O'maks of fwok live rund here.'.*

Mam mother.

Man thy sel! act like a man.

Mannish manage. **Mannisht** *C* managed.

Manny *C, SW* many.

Map'm *C, E, SW,* **Mappen** *C, SW* may happen.

Marcy mercy.

Marra to match; a friend or partner *'H's me marra.';* an equal; marrow.

Marra to bran much alike; a match

for; equal to.

Marraless not alike; not having a friend or partner.

Marras two or more alike; friends or partners.

Marvel marble.

Marypwort *NW* Maryport.

Mash *C, E* mess; to bruise; to crush.

Mash to infuse. *'Mash t'tea, well lass.'.*

Mass *C* to infuse. *'Wilta mass t'tea well fray us, dowter.'.*

Matter an undefined number. *'A matter o'twenty or mair.'.*

Matterable *C* of consequence; important. *'What he does is nivver matterable.'.*

Matterless unimportant. *'Thee teals is matterless, I's still gitten wed.'.*

Matters nothing special; or to boast of. *'nea girt matters.'.*

Mattha *C* Matthew.

Mawse *SW* mouse..

Mayn't may not.

Mayzel *C, SW* to make stupid or stupify; deprive of sensesibility or understanding.

Mead, **Meadd** made.

Meak *SW*, **Meakk** *C, SW* make. *'I's meakkin' yer a churry ceakk.'*; sort.

Meakk on to be kind to; make on; go on.

Meakk out to progress. *'How is he meakkan' out?'.*

Meal, Meall a meal.

Mear *SW*, **Mearr** more.

Measst *C, E, SW* most.

Mebby may be. *'Mebby we'll see Jack agin on Setterday.'.*

Med *C, SW* might. **Med n't** *C, SW* might not.

Meean *SW* mean.

Meeda *C, N, E* meadow.

Meeght *N* might. **Meeght n't** *N* might not.

Meen *C* to moan; bemoan or lament; to express sorrow.

Meent meant, did mean.

Meer more; mare.

Meet *N* might.

Mek *N, E* make; sort or style.

Mell *C* meddle; to interest oneself in the affairs or concerns of others. *'He'll nowder mell nor mak'* - he will not interfere.

Men *N*, **Mend** *C, SW* amend. **Mends** amends. *'He's at t'height of his 'mends '*- nothing more to be given or had.

Meng *N* to renew or refill.

Menna *N* must not.

Menny many. *'He's stopped at heamm menny a neet.'.*

Meooldy mouldy.

Meoor *N* moor.

Mess confusion. *'He hez mead a mess on 't!'.*

Mester *SW* master, mister; teacher. *'T'curate was t'skool mester too.'.*

Meud *C, E, SW*, **Meudd** *C, SW* mud,.

Meuthy weather *E* mild and damp weather.

Meutt ho' moot hall. A town hall, as formerly at Keswick, Cockermouth, etc.

Mew mowed. *Jack mew'd t'meeda wid oald Bob.'*; a mow of corn or hay.

Mey *NW* my.

Meyle *N, NW* mile.

Meynd *NW* remember. (see Mind).

Meyne, **Meyre** *NW* mire.

Meyse *NW* mice.

Mezzer *C, E, SW* measure; measurement.

Mickle much.

Mickle what *C* much the same. *'She's mickle what, parlish feckless.'.*

Middlin' middling or in between; only middling. *'I's gaily weel to-day, but I was nobbet varra middlin' yisterday.'.*

Min man. - only really pronounced when speaking familiarly or with contempt, *'Thou's nea girt things, min.'.*

Mind inclination. *'I've a reet good mind to gang an' tell them.'.*

Mind *SW* remember. *'Mind and think on.';* he does not care *'He duz n't mind'.*

Minny *N* mother.

Minsh mince, *'Git yer minsh pies med for yuletide.'.*

Missled lost, mislaid.

Mist *C* Missed. **Mistakken** *C, N, SW* mistaken. **Mistean** mistaken. **Misteann** mistaken.

Mitch *SW* much.

Mither *N* mother.

Mizzer *N* measure; measure-ment.

Mizzle *C* small or fine rain, drizzle.

Mizzle go away. *'It's gittan leatt an'I mun mizzle.'* .

Moam *C* mellow, soft.

Moithy *E* moist.

Molligrubs *C* bad temper; imaginary ailments; in the sulks. *'She's in t'molligrubs to-day.'.*

Monney *N* many.

Monnish *G, not E* money.

Monny *N* many.

Mooat *SW* must not.

Moon't *C* must not.

Moose *C, N* mouse *'I saw a speckel't la'al moose on yer drisser top.'.*

Morgidge mortgage.

Morrnin' *SW* morning.

Mort *C* a great quantity. *'A mort o'fine things.'.*

Mowerkin *C* Mockerkin.

Muck wet very wet; perspiring copiously *'Dick's muck wet wi'sweat.'.*

Muckle *N* much.

Muckment anything dirty. *'A heap o'muckment.'.*

Mud *C, SW* might. **Mud n't** *C, SW* might not.

Mudder *C, E, SW* mother.

Mug *C* the mouth or face: a fool..

Muggy weather *C* damp and misty.

Mummel to speak low and indistinct; to mumble.

Mump *C* to sulk. *'I ken yer meanin' by yer mumpin'.'*

Mun must.

Munge *C* to grumble in a low tone.

Munkister *SW* Muncaster, near Ravenglass.

Munnet *C* must not.

Mure moor.

Mush *C* to crush; dry crumbling refuse.

Musharam mushroom or fungi.

Musty *C* sour-looking or gloomy; a smell of something damp and unaired.

Mwornin' *C, NE* morning.

Mwort *N* a great quantity. *'A mwort o'fine things.'.*

Myld *C* mile.

Mysen myself.

N't *C* not. *'I'll mebby n't see Jack agin.'.*

Na no.

Naa *N* no, nay.

Nab *C* arrest; to catch suddenly. *'Jwohnny nabb't t'theeaf afwore he legg'd it.'.*

Naebody *N* nobody.

Nag *N* always fault finding. *'Whats yer naggan at now?';* a horse.

Nap *C* to strike gently and quickly.

Nar near. *'To kirk the nar, to God more far.'*

Nar-er, Narder nearer, nearest.

Narer *G, not E* nearer.

Narvish nervous. *'Iv'rybody's narvish when yer git wed.'.*

Nash, Nashy *C, SW* fragile, brittle, tender.

Nastment *E* filth, nastiness.

Nater nature; human feeling or commiseration. *'He hes n't a bit o'nater for nowder dog nor man.'.*

Natterable *C, N* natural.

Nattle to make a light; quick knocking. *'He nattel't at t'window.'.*

Nattral *C* natural.

Natty *C* neat.

Naud *E* strange.

Naww *SW* now.

Nawwt *SW* nothing.

Nay say refusal or denial.

Nayber *C, SW, E* neighbour.

Nayder neither.

Nea no, nay (denial or refusal).

Nea body nobody. *'Nea body likes t'oald goat.'.*

Neaa *SW* no, nay.

Neabody *C, E* nobody.

Neah *C* no.

Neah *C, E, SW* no, nay.

Neak't , Neakk't naked. *'Jack was stark neakk't in t'watter.'.*

Neam, Neamm name.

Nean, Neann *N* none.

Near hand near or close to. *'If you gang near hand you dog it'll bite.'.*

Nearder *G, not E* nearer, nearest.

Neb the bill of a bird; nose; peak of a cap; projecting hill; end, etc.

Nebber *C, SW* neighbour.

Neckin' prolonged sessions of kissing usually between young couples.

Nee *N* no, nay.

Neeadles *SW* needles.

Neeak *SW* nook, corner.

Neean *SW* none; noon, lunch-time.

Neeght *N* night.

Neekkt *C* naked.

Neen *N* nine.

Neer ak *C* never mind.

Neest *C, N* next.

Neest *N* nightest; next.

Neet *C, E, SW* night.

Neeze sneeze.

Ner *C* nor. *'Nowder mair ner less.'.*

Ner nor; than. *'My meer can trot faster ner thine.*

Ner *N* near.

Nerrer *N* nearer, nearest.

Nesh *N* fragile, brittle, tender.

Nessle nestle; as in a nest. *'Nes'lan' abed till past neunn.'.*

Neuk, Neukk *C, N* nook, corner.

Neun *C, N, E,* **Neunn** *C, N* noon, lunch-time.

Newdel 't bewildered; confused through excessive drinking. *'Jonty's newdel't wid yal an' fell't down t'cellar steps.'.*

Newe *SW* new. (pronounced *'nay-oo',* in some parts *'nu'*).

Neyne *NW* nine.
Nieber *N* neighbour.
Niggel't *C* bothered; annoyed.
Nigler *C* a busy, industrious person or animal.
Nim *C* to walk or run with short and quick steps.
Nit *C, SW* not.
Nitch *N* gang, family, or set. *'They're a bad nitch, the heall lot o'them.'.*
Niver, Nivver never. **Nivver let wit** keep it secret; take no notice.
Nobbet nothing but, *'Mary's nobbet a slape clogs.';* only.
Nockles knuckles.
Noddle *C* the head; to nod.
Noo now. *'I hev' the noo.'*- I comprehend.
Noppy *C* tidy, neat. *'Eye, a varra noppy laal body.'.*
Nought at o' nothing at all.
Nought to crack on nothing to boast of.
Nowder neither.
Nowt *C* nothing; zero. **Nowt n'summat** nothing or anything, *'T'oald hag knaa's nowt n'summat.'.*
Nowte nothing. *'I lost nowte when I selt t'oald horse.'.*
Nowther *N* neither.
Nub to nudge; to jog or push secretly or to awaken attention; to butt with elbow or knee.
Num numb; clumsy.
Nut not.
Nut o'theer not all there - silly, foolish or idiotic.
Nut reet not right; idiotic, *'Yer Mary's nut reet in t'heed.'.*
Nwos, Nwose *C* nose. *'His nwos is brock, but yer sud see t'tudder lad.'.*
Nwotice, Nwotis, Nwotish notice.
Nwotion notion; idea. *'Our lad hes a nwotion o'gangan' to sea.'.*
Nwoze nose.
Nyber row *N* neighbourhood; alike with neighbours or others.
O' all, of.
O'riddy *C, E* already. *'I's seen him o'riddy fishing in t'beck.'.*
O'ruddy *N* already.
O't of the. *'This yal hes a tack o't'cask.'.*
O'tha of thee; on thee.
Oa *C* owe, own.
Oal *N* old.
Oalas always.
Oald *C, E* old. *'T'oald church needs a new bell.'.*
Oald fashin't sly; sagacious; precocious; old-fashioned.
Oald lass C an older lady, usually a mother, *'T'oald lass has meadd churry ceakk.*
Oald man father (or occasionally the head of household).
Oalus *C* always.
Oan *G* owe, own. *'Who oans this?'*; to visit. *'Ye nivver oan us.'.*
Obstropolus *C* unruly; turbulent; obstreperous *'He's reet obstropolus.'.*
Occashun *C* occasion.
Od *C* God.
Odments *C* scraps; odds and ends; things worthless, etc.
Ods what difference does it make, what does it matter. *'What ods.'.*
Of'ner *N* more often.
Off an'on *G* uncertain; vacillating; thereabouts. *'When's oald Jwon to come heamm?'....'Off an'on about*

May day.'.

Offcome *C* result or outcome.

Offen often.

Offis *C,* **Offish** office.

Ofner *N* oftener.

Oft *C, E, SW* often. **Ofter** *C, E, SW* more often.

Okart *C, E, N* awkward. *'Divvern't be sea okart.'.*

Olas *C, E* always.

On, Onder under.

Onderhand *C* undersized. *'A laal onderhand creter.'.*

Onny *C, N* any.

Ons *C* puts on. *'I ons wi'my cwoat and off to wark.'.*

Onta on to; upon; unto.

Oor *C, N, E* our; hour.

Oor lass *C* my wife, *'Oor lass is still at heamm wid t'barns.';* our daughter.

Oot out. *'Git oot of yer bed and gaa to wark.'.*

Ootin' *C, N* an outing, a pleasure jaunt or trip.

Ootside outside; at the most. *'He's nobbet six feutt hee et t'oot side.'.*

Op'n, Oppen open. *'Is t'winda op'n ?'.*

Or are. *'Or ye finely?';* ere, before. *'Cuckoo 'll nut come or April.'.*

Other-some *C, SW* other, some other. *'Some flowers is blue, and other-some yallow.'.*

Ours *B* see Oors.

Ov *C* of. *'Safe as the Bank ov Ingland.'.*

Owee come on. *'Owee lets gah to t'Wild Duck at Branthet.'.*

Owder either.

Ower over; to much. **Ower by** *N* over the way. **Owercassen** *N,* **Owergit** *C, SW* overcast.

Ows *N* owns. *'Who ows tis?'.*

Owt anything. *'Mattha was riddy fwor owt' at leukt like fun.';* aught.

Owther *N* either.

Oxters armpits.

Packin be off; go away. *'If thou does n't mind thy wark I'll send thee a-packin', an'seunn teah.'.*

Pacquet *C* the *Cumberland Pacquet* newspaper.

Panceakk *C,* **Pankeakk** pancake. **Panceakk Tuesday** Shrove Tuesday; on which day pancakes are provided for dinner.

Par *C, SW* pair. *I want a par o'new shun.'.*

Pardsah *C* Pardshaw village, near Cockermouth.

Parfet, Parfit perfect.

Parlish *C, SW* wonderful; extraordinary; parlous.

Parral *G, not E* peril. *'It's at te parral to strike.'.*

Parshal *G, not E* parcel.

Past beyond. *'A bad teuthwark's past o'bidin'.'.*

Pat fit; correct; suitable.

Pats *C* the broad wooden blades or paddles used to beat butter into shape before wrapping.

Patter to beat quickly, *'It patters and rains.';* to talk convincingly with confidence. *'H's a greet patter, he'd sell any yan ought.'.*

Pawky *N* too familiar; sly.

Pawwder *SW* powder.

Pawwnd *SW* pound.

Pays *C, N, E* peas.

Paze prize; to prize, or force, or lift with a lever.

Peace appease.
Peaper *C* paper.
Peass, Peazz *C* pace; a raised approach for horses to an upper floor of a farm building.
Peass eggs dyed and boiled eggs handed out at Easter time.
Peasst, Peast paste.
Peav pave.
Peeak *SW* to peek or pry into secret matters. *'He com gloppan' and peeakan' into ivry corner.'.*
Peeal *SW* appeal.
Peeas, Peeaz *SW* peace; peas.
Peel *C, N* appeal. *'I rackan its 'rang to 'peel to court.'.*
Peer *C* poor.
Peer appear; pear; pair *'McAleer at Workiton selt him a peer o'beutts for three bob.'.*
Pelt *C* to throw, separately or in a great number or amount. *'T'lads pelt'd the lasses with sno'balls.'.* **Pelter** *C, N* a large one.
Pen'orth *C* a pennys worth of, or as much as you can buy for a penny. *'I want a pen'orth of treeacle taffy.'.*
Pennerth pennyworth.
Pent paint.
Perfit *N* perfect.
Perlang belong. *'Whee perlangs this?'.*
Peur *N, E* poor.
Peye *N* pie; pye.
Peype *N, NW* pipe.
Pez *C, N, E* peas.
Pick at to invite a quarrel. *'They're always pickin' at yan another.'.*
Picky *E* of weak appetite; fussy.
Pinch't *C* falling short. *'He'll be pinch't to git it done.'.*
Plat *NE* to walk heavily, plod.
Play't *C* played.
Pleas, Pleass place.
Pleass *C* please.
Pleean *SW* to complain.
Pleeasant *N* pleasant.
Pleeaz *SW* please.
Pleen *C, N* to complain.
Pleesant *N* pleasant.
Pleeshur, Pleezer *N* pleasure.
Pleezter more pleased.
Pleukk *N* a pimple on the face.
Pleutery *NE* useless things; refuse. *'Rid away that pleutery, Maggy.'.*
Pleyn *C, N* to complain.
Plezzer *C, SW* pleasure.
Plimlan' *C* the parish and village of Plumbland.
Plizzant pleasant.
Plizzer *E, NW* pleasure.
Plode *C* to wade through thick and thin, plod; work relentlessly.
Plook see Pleukk.
Plote *C* see Plode.
Plyace *C* place.
Pod *C* to poke or prod.
Pode *C* uphold. *'Aa'l 'pode ta it's true.'.*
Poll the head of a person; a register or list of 'heads', that is of persons. eg. at election time.
Pon very commonly used for upon. *'Pon my word.'.*
Pooar *SW* poor.
Pooder *C* hurry, *'Off he went in sec a pooder!';* **Pooder** *C, E,* **Poother** *N* powder.
Pop *C* a dot.
Porpas *SW* purpose.
Portinskeal Portinscale village, near Keswick.

Pot *C, E, SW* has put; did put. **Pot't** *SW* put it.

Pots crockery, dishes and cooking utensils. *'Oor lass has wesh'd the pots.'.*

Potter, Pottle to trifle; to work without any real effect.

Power a great deal. *'It's done him a power o'good.'.*

Preese *C* to press; to importune or request with urgency. *'Aa's preezin' her for an answer.'.*

Prent print, *'T'weddin nwotish war prent'd in the Pacquet.'.* **Prentin'** printing. *'T'prentin in this beukk's varra la'al.'.*

Presarve *C* preserve.

Preuf proof. **Preuve** , **Preuvv** prove.

Preyce *NW* price.

Preyd *NW* pride.

Prin *N* a pin.

Priss *C, SW* to press.

Prizzent present. **Prizzently** presently.

Prush , **Pruss** *C, SW* to press.

Pruzzent *G, not E* present. **Pruzzently** presently.

Pulpot pulpit in a church or chapel.

Pun *C* pin.

Pun *C, N* pound, *'Fwoortin puns to yan steann.'.*

Punchis *C* purchase; the mechanical advantage of a lift or pull. *'He"nivver git it up, because he can't git a purchis at it.'.*

Pund *C, E* a pound in money; a pound, the former measure containing 16 ounces. (equates to approx 454 grams).

Purmit *C* permit.

Put on hurry on; go quick; to tease; to take advantage of.

Put out ashamed, troubled, extinguished. *'Nelly was sair put out about it.'.*

Put tee reets *N* to keep orderly or in a tidy correct manner.

Putten put. *'Yon steann wall badly putten togidder.'.*

Pwok *C,* **Pwoke** a poke; a bag. *'Nivver buy a pig in a pwoke'* - examine first; take nothing on trust.

Pworch porch.

Pwort *E, NW* port. *'Ey, Marypwort.'.*

Queerly *C* odd. *'A rayder queerly swort o'chap.'.*

Quentance acquaintance.

Queyt *N* quite.

Quilt *C* to beat.

Quishin cushion.

Quit rid of; the act of leaving. *'He's quit t'farm and gaan to sea.';* acquit.

Quits *C* even; the share of the bill, *'Lets gaa quits.'.*

Quittance receipt or acquittance. *'Aa'll nit pay yer a penny without a 'quittance.'.*

Raa row. *'Workinton's nobbet raa upo raa of laal hooses.'.*

Raa *N, SW* raw. **Raaish** *N, SW* rather raw.

Rack'nin reckoning. **Rackan** reckon; calculate.

Rackle *C* rash, unruly, incau-tious.

Rackon reckon; calculate; disapprove. *'I rackon nought o'sek wark.'.*

Raft *C* a large concourse, meeting or assembly. *'A raft o'fwok.'.*

Rageous *C, N, E* outrageous.

Rak rake.

Ram to rush; to use force. *'Ram it!'* -

to butt.

Rammel ramble.

Rang wrong. *'Yer fadder thinks yer nivver rang.'.*

Range *C, B* ring; to exercise a young horse in a ring.

Rank close together; numerous. *'As rank as mice in a meal kist.'.*

Ranty *C* riotous; in high spirits; in a towering passion.

Ratch to ramble; to ransack vigorously. *'Ratchan' about like a hungry hound.'.*

Rawwl *C* to grumble; to be quarrelsome.

Rawwnd *SW* round; a circuit.

Rayder *C, SW,* **Raything** *N* rather; ironically very, *'Rayder o't'wettest.'* - very wet.

Reace race.

Reamm *C* to roam; to talk wildly; to covet or desire. *'He's olas reamman efter mair land.'.*

Reap, Reapp rope.

Rear *C* rise, raise; rally; bring up; underdone; nearly raw.

Reass *C,* **Reasses** *N* race or races.

Reatt wrote. *'Thomas Farrell reatt Betty Wilson's Cumm-erland Teals.'.*

Reavvel *C* to use loose talk in a quick manner; to utter untruths; to entangle; to unravel the loops or knitting.

Reaz, Reazz arise, arisen.

Reckon think or work it out.

Redchester register.

Ree-a-zan *SW* reason.

Reed red; to read; to strip. Butchers reed the entrails of slaughtered animals to obtain the fat.

Reeght *N* wright.

Reep up to refer often to some unpleasant subject.

Reet right.

Reet up to put things right; to give scolding advice.

Reg'lar, Reggylar *C,* **Reglar** *N* regular. **Reggalate** regulate.

Remembert *C* remembered.

Repwort report.

Resk *G, not E* risk.

Reud *G, not E,* **Reudd** *C, N* rode; rood, rod or perch - a former measure of land etc.

Reuf *G, not E,* **Reuff** roof.

Reut *C, E,* **Reutt** *C, N* root; to uproot; grub up. *'Reuttan like an unrung swine.'.*

Reyle *N* to vex; to annoy.

Reyme *NW* rhyme.

Rid *G, not E* red.

Riddy ready.

Ridsom' *C* ready; expert.

Rife *C* plentiful.

Rin *N* run.

Ringe *C, E,* **Rinje** rinse.

Rissel *G, not E* wrestle.

Rist rest; repose. *'Rist ye a bit.'..*

Rive to tear; to vomit; to eat voraciously.

Riz *G, not E* arose, arisen.

Ron *C* did run.

Roo *SW* row with oars.

Rooad *SW* road.

Rooar *SW* roar.

Room *C* instead of. *'He com in t'rooms of his fadder.'.*

Roon' *N,* **Roond** *C, E* round; a circuit. *'Aa've been a lang roon' to-day.'.*

Roostit *C, E* rusted.

Rost *C, N, SW* roast.

Rouser a large one. *'It's a roosan lee at is 't.'.*

Rowe *C, E* raw.

Rowl roll.

Rowm *SW* room.

Rozzel *C* to beat. *'Aa'l rozzel thy back wid an esh stick.'.*

Rozzel *C, SW* resin; to heat strongly before a fire. *'Come in an' rozzel thy shins a bit.'.*

Ruck *C* the chief part; the majority.

Ruckle *C* a crowd; a great number.

Ruckshin *C* riot or disturbance. *'There was a reet ruckshin when he came heam last neet.'.*

Rud *G, not E,* **Ruddle** *C* red. **Rudden** ridden.

Ruddy *C, E* ready. **Rudsom'** *E* ready; expert.

Rug *C* to pull rudely. *'Rug at it, lad.'.*

Ruinate *C* to reduce to ruin.

Rum droll; queer. *'He's a rum an'.'.*

Rum or Run butter *C* butter and sugar mixed with spices and flavoured with rum. Traditionally eaten by wives during their confinement; and offered to, and expected to be partaken of, by visitors.

Rumpas disturbance. *'They kick't up a rumpas.'.*

Russel to wrestle.

Rust *G, not E* rest; repose.

Rwoad *C, N, E* road.

Rwoar *C, N, E* roar.

Rwor *C* roar. *'He com rworan like a girt bull.'.*

Rwosy rosy; ruddy; a rose.

Sa so, *'It was sa nasty, it was fit to set a dog.'.*

Saan't *SW* shall not.

Saasiter *N, SW* sausage, *'Cummerlan saasiter fra Wabberthet.'.*

Saat *N, SW* salt.

Sad sodden; pasty; bad. *'She's in a sad way.'.* **Saddan** a sad or bad one.

Sae *N* so.

Sal shall. **Sal n't** *C* shall not. **Sallant** *C, E* shall not.

San' *N* sand.

Sanna *N, E* shall not. **Sannat** *N, E* shall not.

Sap, Sappy wet, rainy.

Sare sore; very much. *'He's sare worn.'.*

Sarious *SW* remarkable. *'It's a sarious fine day.'*

Sark a shirt.

Sarten certain. **Sartenty** certainly. *'Nay, I could n't say for a sartenty.'.*

Sarv't *C* served, *'Furst come furst sarv't.'.* **Sarvice** service.

Savver taste or smell; savour. *'It teasts oald savvor't.'.*

Sawwnd *SW* sound.

Say *C, N* authority, influence. *'He hes full say ower o'.'.* **Sayen** *N* saying.

Scop to hit; to throw.

Scovver *N* discover.

Scowp to empty out or throw away; throw; scoop; scope

Scrabble *B,* **Scribble** *C* to scrawl or write poorly with a pen on paper.

Scram *C, SW* food; once common for the hard rid of bacon or cheese.

Scroby *C* mean, niggardly.

Scrowe *B* a great many. *'A scrowe o'fwok were at t'berryin.'.*

Scut *C* scud, flee or fly with haste; to

make short runs. *'He can scut and run gaily fast til his dinner.'.*

Scworn scorn.

Sea, Seah so.

Seah *SW* sea.

Seak, Seakk sake.

Seal , **Seale** *C* sale.

Seame *C,* **Seamm** same.

Seapp soap.

Searr sore; very much. *'He's sare worn.'.*

Seaskeall *C* Seascale.

Seavv save, *'A tack i'time seavvs nine.'.* **Seavv'd yer bacon** to escape harm. *'Tell yer fadder I seavv'd yer bacon, yer oald lass will nivver finnd out.'.*

Seb'm, **Sebben** *C, E, SW* seven.

Sec such. **Sec a ta-dea** *C* Such a too do, a suprising and eventful happening, often with an unhappy result. *'Yer fadder's furst weddin' was sec a ta-dea.'.*

Secint *N* second.

Seck-like such-like.

Sed said.

See to visit. *'You mun co' to see us when you come our way.'.*

Seeah! *C* see you!

Seean *SW* soon.

Seeat *SW* seat.

Seed *C, N* saw; did see. *'I seed him hoddin her han' in church.'.*

Seeght *N* sight; sigh. **Seeghty** *N* sighty; far-seeing; prudent.

Seein' glass *N* a mirror.

Seek sick.

Seesta see there or look!

Seet sight, *'It was a grand seet to see.'* (older people pro-nounced it *'seeght'* in 1878).

Seeven *N* seven.

See Yers *C* goodbye.

Sel self, *'Behave yer sels.'.*

Selt sold. *'He's selt t'oald picture to a dealer fra Cockermuth.'.*

Sen *C, E, SW* since.

Sen' *N* send. *'Sen' the cat out, hizzy.'.*

Sennat *C* seven nights; a week.

Serious remarkable. *'Ey, it's serious het an'all.'.*

Set to appoint; to fix, *'He's set a day for the weddin'.'*; to plant; to equal; to escort, to accompany; to suffer or allow. *'She fell asleep and set t'fire out.'*; nauseous. *'It was sa nasty, it was fit to set a dog.'.* **Set a feass** *C* to gurn or distort the human face. **Set by** put to one side; held in esteem, *'He's girtly set by hereaway.'.* **Setfast** secure and virtually impossible to move. **Setten** *C* appointed; commenced. *'Mary's setten up shopkeepin' in Workinton.'.*

Setterday Saturday.

Seun *C, E, N,* **Seunn** *C* soon. *'We'll seunn be wed lass.'.*

Seur *N, SW,* **Seurr** *N* sure.

Seyde *NW* side.

Seyn, **Seyne** *N* since.

Shak *C, N, E, SW* shake, a shaking, shook or shaken.

Shakes *W* nothing special; or to boast of. *'H's nea girt shakes.'.*

Shap *C, E* shape.

Shavvins *C* shavings.

Shawwer *SW* shower.

Sheak, Sheakk *C, N* shook; shaken; shake it.

Sheam, Sheamm shame; be ashamed.

Sheap *E, SW,* **Sheapp** *SW* shape.
Sheavins *N* shavings.
Sheear *SW* share.
Sheeers *N* scissors.
Shem *N* shame; be ashamed of.
Shep *N* shape.
Sheuk *C, E,* **Sheukk** shook.
Sheyn *NW* shine.
Shift *C, N* to remove.
Shill to shell; to unshell; cold, chill. **Shill out** pay. *'Yer fadder will nivver shill out for t'weddin.'.*
Shillies *C* shore gravel or small stones.
Shippert shepherd.
Shive a slice; a cut.
Shodders *C* shoulders.
Shoo *C* shoe. **Shoo swol** *C* shoe sole.
Shooar *C, N, E* shower; *SW* shore. *'Let's ga dawwn to t'shooar an'hev a dook.'.*
Shooder shoulder. **Shooder spaw** *N* the shoulder-blade.
Shool *C, N, E* shovel.
Shoon *N* shoes.
Shoor *C, E* sure.
Shoot *C, N, E* shout; to cry out; to call.
Short tongue't said of one who lisps.
Shot did shut; a half-grown swine; the share of the bill eg. at an inn etc; quit; rid of. *'Yer should git shot of t'oald yowe.'*; broken, damaged, in need of repair. *'That oald cart is well shot.'.*; the worst.
Shottel *N* schedule.
Shuk *C* shook.
Shun *C, E* shoes.
Shwort *NW* short.
Shyve *C, N* a slice. *'Cut thy sel a shyve o'cheese an' breed.'.*
Sidders *C, E, SW* scissors.
Side up to put things to their places. **Sidement** a putting of things to their places. *'We nobbet skiftit here this week an'hes n't gitten a sidement yet.'.*
Sidlins *N* in the neighbourhood. *'He's geann to t'sidins o'Caarel.'.*
Sight a great number or quantity. *'Theer was a sight o'fwok at Rosley fair.'.*
Simmer *N* summer.
Simmon't cemented.
Sin, Sin-syne *N* since.
Sing-el *C, E* single.
Sista *C, SW* look; see thou; seest thou.
Sitten sat. *'She'd sitten o't'efterneunn.'.*
Sizel *C* to saunter or wander about idly; to loiter or linger.
Skeap *C, E,* **Skeapp** escape.
Skearce scarce.
Skeery scry, wild, feary.
Skeul *C, E N* school.
Skilly *N* skilful; having skill. *'He's gay an' skilly at his trade.'.*
Skint short of money; skinned.
Skitters diarrhoea.
Skleat *N, E,* **Skleatt** *N* slate.
Skons *N* scones.
Skooal *SW* school.
Skooar score.
Skraffle *C* to scramble; dispute; struggle. *'He's hed a sare skraffle for a leevin', an' he skraffles an' disputes wid ivry body.*
Skratt rake.
Skrimpy scanty; mean; pinched hospitality.

Skruf o' t'neck the nape or back of the neck *'Jack grabbed him by t'skruf o' t'neck.'*.

Skrunty dwarfish or small; worn, *'A skrunty besom'* - one far worn.

Skurry *C* bustling hurry.

Slaa *N, SW* slow.

Slak slack or loose; small pieces of coal under the size of an egg.

Slank *N* to walk away abjectly.

Slant to tell untruths.

Slashy wet and dirty.

Slatter to spill; childish play in water. **Slattery** raining or showery weather.

Slavver slobber, saliva.

Sleat, **Sleatt** slate. *'Yer git green sleatt fray Borrowdale.'*. **Sleatt lowse** somewhat lunatic or mad.

Slee *N* sly.

Sleep't *C, E* slept.

Slevver *N* slobber, saliva.

Slew *C* to turn partly round. *'Slew that kist round a bit.'*.

Slew't *C* partly intoxicated.

Sling to move by long and steady strides. *'He slings ower t'grund at a girt rate.'*.

Slinge *C* to walk away abjectly.

Slip to slide; to go quickly and quietly. *'Slip away for some watter, lass.'*; a child's pinafore.

Slobber *C* to weep with many tears. *'He slobber't an' yool't like a barn.'*.

Slowp *C, E* slope.

Slysh *SW* a slice. *'Cut thy sel a slysh o'keeak.'*.

Smaa *N, SW* small.

Smeeak *N, SW* smoke. **Smeuk** *C, N, E* smoke.

Smeeth *C* smooth.

Smiddy smithy.

Smithers *C* small fragments. *'It was o'broken to smithers.'*.

Smo *C, E* small.

Sna *C, N, SW* snow. **Snaat** *SW* snowed.

Snaffle *C* to steal. **Snaf' lan'** trifling; petty pilfering. *'T'Wallace lads are saf'lan' oald Jonty's apples.'*.

Snap't up to eagerly acquire everything on offer. *'Dick snap't up all t'oald beukks at t'sale.'*.

Snappy *C* short-tempered. *'Yer Marys a reet snappy lass at present.'*.

Sneck the latch or catch on a door or gate; a hitch or stop.

Snews *N* snooze, half-sleeping.

Snick *C* a minor clip or cut; to clip a sheep, etc., in uneven ridges.

Snife *C* knife.

Snifter *C* to inhale sharply through the nostrils; quickly done, *'In a snifter.'*.

Sno'an snowing. *'It's been sno'an hard sen Setterday.'*.

Snoor *SW* snore.

Snotter *C, N* to blubber. *'Snotter an' yool.'*; small particles in paint etc. when decorating.

Snotty mean, disagreeable. *'He's a laal snotty cur of a fellow.'*.

Snwoar *C, N, E* snore.

Soft soder flattery.

Somewhoars somewhere.

Sook *C, E* suck.

Soom *N* swim. *'Can ta soom any?'*.

Soond *C, E* sound.

Soop *C* to sweep. **Soop't** *N* swept.

Sooth south.

Sositer *C* sausage, *'Woodall's mak reet teasty Cummerlan sositer.'.*

Sowe to sew.

Sowjer *N* soldier.

Sowt *N* sought, brought.

Spak *C, E, SW* spoke, spake.

Span new *C* brand new, never having been used.

Spanker a tall and active young person; something very special; a fast-going horse. **Spankin'** *C* a beating.

Spar spare, save.

Spead spade. **Speadd** spade.

Speak, **Speeak** *C, E, SW* spoke, spake.

Speatt *C* a sudden and heavy fall of rain; a water-spout. *'A speatt o'rain.'.*

Spell a chip; a small splinter of wood'; a turn of work, etc. *'Let's tak a spell at kernin'.'.*

Speshul *C* special.

Speun *C, N, E,* **Speunn** *C, NE* spoon.

Speyse *NW* spice.

Spit When the warning drops of a shower fall. *'It rayder spits.'.*

Spok *N* spoke, spake. **Spok'n** spoken. **Spokkan** spoken.

Sponsible responsible, *'It's nivver her 'sponsilblity.';* sub-stantial.

Spooan *SW* spoon.

Spot *C* a position or place; a place of service. *'I gang to my spot at Martinmas hirins.'.*

Spreead *SW* to spread. **Spreed** *C, N, E* to spread.

Spurt to increase the pace you are working or walking etc.

Spwort sport.

Spy'd *C* saw. *'I spy'd them hand in hand down t'beck.'.*

Stack stuck. *'He stack in a t'mud.'.*

Stakker stagger. *'He stakker't a bit an' than he fell't ower efter all that yal.'.*

Stand cost. *'Them lambs 'll stand me in laal short of a pund a piece.';* the large washing-tub in which the dolly is worked.

Stank *C* stink or bad smell. *'T'hoose stank to high heaven.';* to groan short. *'Stankan' and greannan' as if he ail't summat.'.*

Stap stave of a tub; step of a ladder or gate; become insolvent, *'Tom's gone o'to staps.'.*

Stashin *C* station.

Stead *SW* stood. **Steadd** stood.

Stean stone. **Steann** stone.

Steeak *SW* stuck.

Steeal *SW* steel; steal; stool; to tiller; to spread in growing.

Steeam *SW* steam.

Steepin' rain heavy pen-etrating rain.

Steud *C, E, N* stood. **Steudd** stood, did stand.

Steul *C, N, E* stool. **Steul** *N* stole. **Steull** *C, N* stool; to tiller; to spread in growing; *N* stole.

Stew *C, N* excitement; haste. *'In a girt stew.'.*

Stick up for to advocate or support. *'He stack up weel for Tom.'.*

Stickle *C* fright; alarm. *'In a parlish stickle.'.*

Stinjy *C* miserly; unlikely to freely to part with anything.

Stint *C* a measure of work; in coalmines an area 2 yards long by 1 yard broad, which each miner clears removing to another place (equates to approx 1.67 square metres).

Stir *C* bestir, exert or rouse. *'Stir thy feet, Bob.'*; excitement.

Stob stab; a post or stake.

Stoop *N, SW* a gate-post; the turning-post in a race.

Stop to stay; to stow or pack. *'Stop them things into t'drawer.'*.

Stown stolen.

Strang strong. *'Jennings mak varra strang yal at Cockermuth.'*; fetid, strong or rancid scent. *'Strang as rotten cheese.'*.

Strapp't short of money. *'Dicks a laal bit strapp't efter t'weddin.'*.

Streen to strain, press or make great effort; sprain; distrain.

Street straight. **Streetan** straight; straighten. **Streight** straight.

Strenth strength.

Streyk *NW* strike.

Streyve *NW* strive.

Strinkle sprinkle. **Strinklin'** sprinkling.

Stroppan' strapping; tall; active, *'Yer Jack's a reet stroppan lad.'*.

Studden *C, E* stood, *'Thou sud ha'studden up for us.'*.

Stumps legs, *'Stir yer stumps.'*.

Stwory story. *'Varra weel than, to mak a lang stwory short.'*; an untruth.

Su did sow; did sew; to sew. *'He su his cworn yisterday.'*; a sow or female swine.

Sud should, *'Thou sud ha'studden up for us.'*. **Suddent** sudden; should not.

Sugger sugar.

Sum *C* some.

Summat something; somewhat. **Summat-like** something like or adequate for the purpose; pretty or becoming. *'Theer, that's summat-like!'*.

Sunday best the best outfit in your wardrobe, once general y worn to attend church on a Sunday.

Sup to sip; to take liquid food from a spoon; an indefinite measure of liquids. *'A girt sup.'*, *'A laal sup.'*, *'A sup o'tea.'*. **Supping** *C* drinking.

Suppwose suppose.

Swadder *C* to dabble or play in water. *'Swadderan' like a duck in a puddle.'*.

Swally to swallow.

Swanky *C* loosely put together; inferior; showy or conceited actions, speech or dress.

Swattle *C, N* to waste; to sip intoxicating beverages.

Swayvel to walk unsteadily.

Sweet perspiration or sweat.

Swelter *C, N* to perspire copiously. *'O'in a swelter.'*.

Swet *C, E, SW* did sweat.

Swey *C, N, E* swing, sway.

Swidder *C* to shiver with cold. *'O'in a swidder.'*.

Swig *C* a long drink. *'Oald Dick could swig a quart at a wind.'* .

Swoak soak.

Swober sober.

Swok soak.

Swol *C* sole of the foot, shoe, etc.

Swolly to swallow.

Sworry sorry. **Swory** sorry.

Swort sort; to select; to arrange.

Swuft swift, rapid.

Swum *C* swim. *'Can ta swum ower*

t'Derwent?'.

Sydle *C, N* to saunter; to approach sideways or obliquely in a fawning or coaxing manner.

Syne *N* since.

Syte a great deal. *'A syte o'fwok.'.*

Syzel to saunter; to trifle.

T *C, SW* the.

T'laal an *C* the little one; the child. *'Emilly's t'laal an in ma hoose.'.*

T's it *C* it is it; that is it.

Ta thee, thou; thanks; to or too.

Ta *SW, NW* tall.

Ta-dea *C, SW* to do.

Taa thanks.

Taak *N, SW* talk.

Tack *N* a stitch, *'A tack i'time seavvs nine.'.*

Taffy *C* toffy or toffee. *'Margaret Marsh's laal shop in Powe Street selt taffy and mint marbles.'.*

Tagidder *C* together.

Tak *C, SW* take; a trick or lift in card-playing. **Takkan** *C, SW* taking; infection. **Tak efter** to resemble. *'Jack hes rid hair and taks efter t'fadder fworsuer.'.*

Tak up wid to associate with. *'He's tak'n up wid her fray Eggermouth.'.*

Tan to beat. *'Yer fadder will tan his hide for him.'.*

Tarm *N* term.

Tarrable *N* terrible; This word is also often used to indicate something extraordinary eg. *'tarrable nice', 'tarrable hee', "tarrable low'* etc.

Tat *C* that, *'Is tat t'reet way t'Workinton?'.*

Tatter hurry. *'In a tatter.'*; to scold. *'She gev him a rare tatteran.'.*

Tatty *N* matted or uncombed; quite worn.

Taty potato. **Taty hash** potato based soup. **Taty pickin'** *C* the time when whole families were employed to pick potatoes.

Tawwn *SW* town.

Taylear tailor.

Te *C, N, SW* to.

Te-enn *N* taken.

Teabbel *C, N, E* table.

Teah *C* too. *'Put t'deer teah '*- close the door.

Teah *SW* tea.

Teak *C, N,* **Teak** *SW,* **Teakk** take, took.

Teal, **Teall** tale; tail.

Tean *C, SW, E* taken. **Teann** *C, SW* taken.

Tearm *N, E* term.

Teasst, **Teast** taste.

Teattit matted, uncombed.

Teaylear *N, NW, E* tailor.

Tee *C* thee, thou. *'Is tat tee, Bobby?'.*

Tee *G, not E* too.

Teeas toes.

Teem to empty; to pour out. *'Bob Elliott teems t'rid hot stile at Workiton's Moss Bay warks.'.*

Teen *N* taken.

Teer *N* there, there is.

Teeram *C, SW* term.

Teethan' teething; getting teeth. *'La'al Jack's not yet teethan'.'.*

Tek *N, E* take.

Tell able to remember and able to tell of. *'He niver h'ard tell on't.'.*

Telt told.

Tem *C, SW* them.

Tetch *C* to be restive or obstinate.

Teu too.

Teuff *C* tough. **Teufish** *C* rather tough.
Teuh *C* to.
Teuk *C, E* took. *'His teuk himsel' off back t'London.'.* **Teukk** took.
Teull tool.
Teun, **Teunn** tune.
Teuth tooth. **Teuthwark** *C, SW* tooth-ache. **Teuthyik** *N* tooth-ache.
Teydy *NW* tidy.
Teym *NW* time.
Teyny *NW* tiny.
Teyt *NW* tight.
Teytel *NW* title.
Thaim *N* them.
Thairty *N* thirty.
Than then. **Than-abouts** about that time.
That so. *'I was that vex't I could ha'bitten t'side out of a butter-bowl.'.*
That'n, **That'un** that one.
Thawwsan' *SW* thousand.
Thay *C* They.
The *C* Thee, thou or you. *'I know the noo.'.*
Thear, Thearr *SW* there, there is.
Theeas *SW* these, those.
Theer *C, N, E* their; there is, there. *'Yer lad's ower theer wid oor lass ageann.'.*
Theesal *C* yourself. *'Hev a thrippenny bit ta treat theesal wid.'.*
Thenk thank.
Thersells *C* themselves.
Theyn thine, belonging to thee etc. *'I'l tak nowt of theyne, when am geann.'.*
Thick *N* familiar, friendly; unthinking or unintelligent. *'Thick as pig shit.'.* **Thick set** low and strongly built. **Thick skin't** not sensitive; unfeeling.
Think on to remember; to keep in mind.
This'n this one; this thing. *'This'n better than that'n.'.*
Thole to endure; to suffer. *'He'll nivver thole the oaldfowk alone.'.*
Thoo's *C, E, N* thou or you. *'Too's nivver gangan to see her ageann.'.*
Thoom thumb.
Thou'l *N, E* thou or you wilt or will.
Thowt, Thowte thought.
Thraa *SW* throw.
Thrang throng; busy. *'Thrang as Botchergeatt ivry Setterday neet.'.*
Thraw throw.
Threeten threaten.
Threshurt *N,* **Threshwurt** *C* threshold.
Thribble treble; three times.
Thrins *C* triplets or three at a birth.
Thrippence Three pence. **Thrippenny bit** a former coin worth three old pence.
Thrist *G, not E* thrust, did thrust.
Throo through; threw or throw.
Throssan *C, E, SW,* **Thrussan** *N* thrust, did thrust; thrusting.
Thrwoat *N* throat.
Thunner thunder.
Thur *C* these; those.
Thurd *C, N, E* third.
Thurrans *C* these ones.
Thurty *C, E* thirty.
Thwaite a cleared space in a wood or wilderness. A very common termination to placenames.
Thwort *C* thought.
Thy adjective of thou; belonging to thee or you; your *'Yer fadder paid*

t'rent and seavv'd thy farm.'.

Ti't *C* tied, bound, obliged. *'He was ti't gang an' ti't to work when he dud gang.'.*

Til't *N* to it.

Till *C, N* to, too. *'Put that dooer till.' 'Is ta gaan till t'market?'.*

Tilt quickly. *'He went full tilt doon bank an'fell an' brak his nwose.'.*

Timmer timber.

Tiry *C* tired, fatigued.

Tis this.

Titty *N* sister. *'Mary's yer titty, nut yer mam.'.*

Tittyvate to put into order; decorate; fit out.

To *C* tall.

To-neet tonight.

Togidder together.

Toller *C* to holler or speak loudly and roughly. *'Tolleran' like a mad bull.'.*

Too *C* thee, thou. **Too'l** *C* thou wilt.

Tooa *C, SW* two.

Tooar tower.

Toon town.

Tooz *C, N* thou art.

Torious *N* notorious.

Torn *SW* turn. *'Ga' rawwnd t'hawwse an' torn that aa'd caww back into t'faald.'.*

Torts *SW* towards.

Tossicatit *N* intoxicated.

Touchy easily offended.

Towerts *C, N, E* towards.

Towple, Toytle to upset; overturn or topple over.

Tread *C, E, SW,* **Treadd** *C, SW* trode.

Tret treat or treated. *'She's been reet badly trettan by him.'.*

Treuth truth.

Trinkle trickle. *'Bleudd com trinklan' down his feass like drops o'rain.'.*

Tripe *C* utter nonsense.

Tu *C* to tease; annoy; struggle. *'He's been a tusom barn.'.*

Tu *SW* too. *'I's frae Oofa tu.'.*

Tudder the other.

Tuk *C, N* took. **Tukkan** *C, SW* taken. *'She's tukkan tul'it varra well.'.*

Tul, Tull to. **Tul't** *C, SW* to it. .

Twaddle unmeaning talk.

Twang an accent; a pang of toothache; the sound of a stringed instrument.

Tweea *N, E* two.

Tweyn *NW,* **Twine** to whine; complain. *'She tweyns an' twists on, peer laal body!';* twist; a course string or rope.

Twitter *C* edge. *'Just in a twitter'* - on the very edge.

Twonty *N* twenty.

Udder *C, E, SW* other.

Um *C* him.

Un one (as in 'baddun' - bad one).

Uppish *C* conceited; holding a high head.

Uptak lifting; finding. *'Aa fand his watch on t'rwoad and he ga'me summat for t'uptak.'.*

Ur *C, N* are. *'Ho ur ye to-day, oor Jack?'.*

Us me. *'Please give us a lift.'.*

Usefuller more useful. *'Tom's mearr usefuller than t'udders.'.*

Varra *C, E, SW* very. *'It's het weather, varra!'.* **Varra nigh** *C* very near. **Varra weel** very well. Often used in relating news, etc. *'Varra weel* *than, I'll tell ye o'about it.'.* **Varry** *N* very.

Varst vast, a great number or quantity.

Ventersom' adventurous, rash.

Vex't *C* irritated; angry; tor-mented.

Wa *C* why, well. *'Wa noo than! '.*

Wa *C, E, SW* with. *'Gang wa Tom.'.*

Wa we. *'We'll gang when wa like.'.*

Waa *SW* wall.

Waareld *C, SW* world.

Wabble wobble or waddle; to rock sideways in walking.

Wad would. *'Wad ta like to len'me a shillin'?'.*

Waffle to waver; to be undecided; to talk incessantly, much of which maybe nonsence.

Wah *C, SW* with.

Wake *C, E, SW* weak.

Walla *C* weak; faint from want or illness; tasteless; insipid.

Wan won, did win.

Wankle weak or feeble. *'Poor Jemmy! he's varra wankle.'.*

Wannel *N* lithe; agile; flexible.

War were. *'War ye ivver at Whitehebm.'.* **War'nt** was not; to assure; warrant. *'Aa's war'nt ta it is.'.*

Wareet right; rarely heard.

Wark ache; work. *'It's slow wark to sup buttermilk wid a pitchfork.'.*

Warld *C, SW* world.

Warm to beat. *'Aa'll warm tha.'*

Warse worse. *'Warse and warse like Worki'ton clark.'.* **Warsen** to grow worse. **Warst** *C* worst.

Was ter? was there; were there.

Wath a ford or crossing through a stream.

Watna *N* do not know. *'I watna what it is.'.*

Watter water. **Watterey like** appearance of rain coming; watery or well diluted. *'This pents varra watterey like.'.*

Wauddent *C* would not.

Waugh *B* a unpleasing scent or smell.

Way *G* used as expressive of comparison or degree; direction or area. *'He leevs someway out Wigton way.'.*

Way betyde ye *N* You'll be getting into trouble.

Wayster a waster; a thief; excrescence in the candle.

Wazzant *C* was not.

We's *SW* we shall. *'We's ga'to Wastle Heead.'.*

We't *E, SW* with it.

We-ans *C, N* children, little ones.

Wear *N, E* wore.

Weary *C* tiresome; monotonous. *'It's a weary rwoad to Warnel fell.'.*

Weast *C* waste; the waist.

Weay *N* woe; pity. *'I's weay for them, poor things! '.*

Weayst *N, E* waste; the waist.

Wedder weather; wether.

Weddin *C* wedding, marriage. **Weddiners** a wedding party. **Weddit** wedded.

Weder weather; wether.

Wee *C, N* little or small. *'Wee Jack cud nivver reach the dresser top.'.*

Weeage *SW* wage.

Weeat *SW* wet, rain.

Weeky *C, N* moist, juicy.

Weel well. *'He stack up weel for t'lass.'.*

Ween't *C, E* will not.

Weet *C, N* wet, rain. *'It weets fast.'.*

Weft *C* to beat. *'Aa'll give him a weftin' some day.'.*

Well *C, E, SW* weld.

Welt *C* to beat.

Wend *C* to turn round.

Went on continued; talked or chatted ceaselessly. *'She went on at a parlish rate.'.*

Wesh *C, N, E* wash.

Wey *C* well, why; notes of assent or dissent. *'Wey, yes.' 'Wey, no.'. 'Wey, Ey'.*

Weyd *NW* wide; wife; wile or deceive; wine.

Weydness *NW* width.

Weysh *SW, NW* wash.

Whaa *SW* who. **Whaa-ivver** *SW* whoever.

Whaar *E, SW* where.

Whack a blow or thwack.

Whang to throw; to hit; a leather shoe-tie; a strap used in stitching a cart-harness; a thong; a lump or large piece. *'A whang o'cheese.*

Whap a blow.

What'n? *N* what? *'What'n clock is 't?'.*

Whatsomivver whatsoever.

Whe *N* who.

Whedder whether.

Whee *N* who.

Whee-ivver, *N, E* whoever.

Wheea *N, E* who. *'Wheea's that?'.*

Wheer *N* where.

Wheezle to breathe with difficulty. *'She wheezles like a pursy horse.*

Wheg *E* a lump or thick slice.

Whel *C* until, *'Stay whel I come back.'.*

Whel *E* while, whilst.

Whets *C* flashes of wit. *'Sec whets we hed tudder neet.'.*

Whew *C* haste. *'Sec a whew he's in!'.*

Whey aye *N* yes, of couse.

Whick quick; alive. *'Git yeamm whick else yer miss her.'.*

Whiet quiet.

Whiff *C* smell, *'I just gat a whiff of t'reek.'*; discover a secret or tale, often through hearing a rumour.

While *C* until, *'Stay while I come back.'.*

Whinge to whine.

Whissel *C, E, SW* whistle.

Whissle *C* whistle; the mouth. *'Weet yer whissle.'.*

Whittle a knife.

Who-ivver *C* whoever.

Whoar *C, E* where.

Whoaraway *C* where. *'Whoaraway hes to been?'.*

Whol whole; hole.

Whopt *C* hoped.

Whup whip.

Whup hand the advantage.

Whussel *N, E* whistle.

Wi *C, E, SW* with. **Wi'am** *SW* with him. **Wi'ma** *C, SW* with me.

Wi'ya *C* will you, *'Wi'ya ivver see us agin or is yer gean for good.'.*

Wid with. **Wid'am** *C* with him. **Wid-out** *C* without; unless. *'He'll hev to gang wid-out her efter aal.'.*

Wideness, Widness *C* width.

Will to bequeath. *'He will't his money to t'dowter.'.* **Wills** *C* doubts. *'Aa's i'wills whether to gang or nit.'.*

Wilta? *C, E, SW* wilt thou or will you?.

Wima *C, E, SW* with me.

Win' *N* wind; to wind. **Wind** *C, E,*

SW wind; to wind; the time occupied in drawing the breath. *'Dick could swallow a quart at a wind.'.*

Windy noisy; talkative. *'Mair wind nor woo' like clippin' a swine.'.*

Windy bags an incessant talker. *'Oor Mary's sec a windy bags.'.*

Winna *N,* **Winnet** *C, E* will not.

Wipe a hint. *'She gives him many a wipe about it.'.*

Wise like *N* wise and prudent.

Wittin' knowledge, intelligence. *'I dud t'best o'my wittin'.'.*

Wizzen't lean or thin, withered or wizened.

Wo' *C, N, E* wall.

Woe betyde yer you'll be getting into trouble.

Wokan awaken, waken.

Woo' wool.

Wor *N* were.

Woremest foremost.

Worriment harassing, annoy-ance.

Wots *B* knows; is aware of.

Wrang wrong. *'It's wrang to wrang ennybody.'.*

Wrap up finish; shut up; desist or give up.

Wreat *C, E* wrote.

Wreyt *NW* write.

Wu'ma *N* with me.

Wud *N* mad; with. **Wud'am** *N* with him.

Wun' *C, N* wound. *'He wun'up his watch.'.* **Wunder** *C* wonder.

Wunna *N* will not.

Wur *N* were.

Wurd word.

Wurl *N* world.

Wut *N* wit.

Wuth *N* with.

Wuvver *B* however; indeed.

Ya *C, SW* one.

Yaak *C, SW* oak.

Yaap *SW* to whoop; to shout.

Yabble *C* able.

Yage *G, not E* age. **Yage** *N* to grow old.

Yah way or anudder *C* One way or the other.

Yal, Yale *C, E, SW* ale. **Yal-jaw't** *C* sickened by drinking ale, drunk. **Yalhoose** inn or public house.

Yalla yellow.

Yalseal *SW* wholesale.

Yam *B* ham.

Yan *C, SW* one. **Ya-day, Yan-day** *C* one day (a common retrospection). *'It was ya-day last week.'.* **Yananudder** *C, E, SW* one another.

Yance *C, E, SW* once. *'I'll try it just yance mair an nivver ageann.'.*

Yar your.

Yat *C, SW* a gate.

Ye *C* You. *'Hoo ur ye?'.*

Ye'r *SW* your; you are.

Yea's *SW* you shall. *'Yea's come, if yers like.'.*

Yel *N, E* ale.

Yella yellow..

Yen *N* one.

Yenaither, Yenanither *N* one another.

Yence *N* once.

Yer your, *'Behave yer sel.'*; you are. **Yers** *W* you, *'Where yers gaan.'.* **Yer sel** yourself. *'Help yer sels to minsh pies.'.* **Yer'l** *C* you will or you'll. *'Yer'l git it on Setterday.'.*

Yerd yard.

Yerth earth.

Yet *N* a gate.
Yin *N* one.
Yis yes.
Yister *C* Yesterday, sometimes seen as *'Yister neet'* - yesterday night.
Yisterday yesterday.
Yit yet.
Yoller *C, N* to shout; to halloo.
Yon over there.
Yooar *C, N, E* your; udder.
Yool *C, N* weep and cry.
Yope *C* to whoop; to shout.
Yub'n *C* oven.
Yucks *N* itches; is tickled.
Yule *N* Christmas.
Yuly yuly *B* a call to bring geese together.
Yungest *N* youngest.
Yungster *C* youngster.
Yurl *B* earl. (see Yerl).
Yurth *N* earth.
Zookers! *C, SW* an exclamation of surprise or admiration.
Zukkers! *C, SW* see Zookers.

Design n' Prent'd in Workin'ton by Pages n' Pages. 1.02